UNCOMMON SENSE

UNCOMMON SENSE

A Layman's Briefing Book on the Issues

Cal Thomas

241
Tho

Wolgemuth & Hyatt, Publishers, Inc.
Brentwood, Tennessee

Wolgemuth & Hyatt, Publishers, Inc.
1749 Mallory Lane, Suite 110
Brentwood, Tennessee 37027.

Library of Congress Cataloging-in-Publication Data

Thomas, Cal.
    Uncommon sense : a layman's briefing book on the issues / Cal
Thomas. — 1st ed.
       p. cm.
   ISBN 0-943497-92-2
   1. Christian ethics. 2. Christianity and politics. 3. Church and
social problems — United States. 4. United States — Politics and
government — 1981-1989. 5. United States — Politics and
government — 1989- 6. Christianity and international affairs.
7. United States — Foreign relations — 1981-1989. 8. United States —
Foreign relations — 1989-   I. Title.
BJ1251.T44 1990
241'.0973'09049 — dc20

                      90-35566
                      CIP

For Ronald Reagan,
whose uncommon sense made him not only
the man of the 1980s,
but whose steadfastness and consistency
brought the triumph of American values and
the defeat of communism,
thus insuring his place in history
as the major figure of the second half
of the twentieth century

CONTENTS

ACKNOWLEDGMENTS

F EW BOOKS ARE ISLANDS, though some are written on them. Even God used a number of human instruments to write His Book. I have used a number of human instruments to help me with mine.

Mike Gerson, who currently works as a speech writer in Washington D.C., contributed essential background material.

My publishers, Robert Wolgemuth and Mike Hyatt, were constant sources of affirmation and encouragement. Never have I met two publishers who follow through on every promise. They are men of integrity in an industry that could use more of that commodity.

My wife, Ray, is a valuable sounding board off of whom I bounce many ideas. Now a successful family counselor, she thinks she has me figured out. Now if I could only figure me out!

The management and editorial staff at the *Los Angeles Times* syndicate is the greatest bunch of people I have ever been associated with in my nearly thirty-year journalism career.

Heartfelt thanks to all of these people!

INTRODUCTION

CURRENT EVENTS are moving so swiftly that they change, not from year to year, not even day to day, but hour to hour. The happenings of 1989 telescoped history more rapidly than perhaps any similar period. Within weeks the Berlin Wall came tumbling down, and within days of that event, Communist leaders of East European governments began resigning.

It is difficult enough for the average person whose business is not news, as mine is, to keep up with what's going on at home and abroad, much less put it in perspective or in historical context.

Yet we cannot afford the luxury of apathy and noninvolvement. Not to be part of the change means that others will be able to dictate the direction and composition of that change, bringing results we might not like. If we do not participate, if we opt out, we will be powerless to reverse any trend. Doing nothing is, in fact, doing something: It often helps the side that holds a view opposite of our own. It leaves one less soldier in the battle, one less person to defend against.

Next to the question, "I'm only one person, so what can I do?" I suppose the question most often asked of me is, "Where can I go, what can I read, to tell me what I need to know about the world?"

The purpose of this book is to familiarize you, from a conservative viewpoint, with the major world and national issues at the beginning of the last decade of the twentieth century. This volume includes columns I have written within the past three years that were syndicated in more than 120 newspapers by the *Los Angeles Times* Syndicate. Interspersed throughout the book are "briefings," which are historical overviews of some of the issues. These are included for those without the time or resources to research questions they need to know about.

I hope that the combination of information and opinion will help you to formulate or undergird your own views and will expand your knowledge and capabilities in discussing these issues with friends and acquaintances.

Thus I would like for this book to serve as a manual, a primer, for those who want to become informed so that they might be more active in the political and social life of our nation. It should be a tool, but a tool will do nothing if it is left in the tool box; it must be used. That's where you come in. May this book help motivate you to use the knowledge you acquire!

The 1990s afford incredible opportunities to redress the ethical, social, and political grievances of the last thirty years. Only a people well informed on the issues can do this.

If this book contributes to the corporate wisdom; if it encourages people to act where they live as salt in their culture; if the example of one conservative determined to penetrate the media with his ideas encourages others to do likewise, I shall feel I have done my part.

PART ONE

ISSUES INTERNAL

★ ★ ★

AMERICA WITHIN ITSELF

AT ISSUE

ABORTION

ABORTION

Abortion is the most volatile issue that has faced America since the Civil War. Not even the Vietnam War divided us for so long. During the Civil War, the issue was whether a nation could endure, in Lincoln's words, "half slave and half free." Now the issue is whether another minority group, preborn children, will be allowed to exist at all and whether we, as a nation, will endure when we continue to slaughter a large percentage of the next generation at the rate of three thousand per day.

It is important to put the abortion issue in perspective. Abortion is the result, not the cause, of the moral and ethical problems we have created for ourselves. Nineteen seventy-three, the year the Supreme Court announced the *Roe v. Wade* decision, followed the turbulent 1960s during which every value and tradition held by the previous generation was overthrown in a bloodless coup.

The blood would come later when the Supreme Court, seeing that there were no longer standards by which right and wrong might be measured (at least none it was willing to recognize), allowed women, and women alone, to make the decision whether to take the lives of their preborn children.

The Court had a lot of help from the press and entertainment industries and from various groups and organizations that benefit from abortion on demand, which is now a multibillion-dollar industry. It happened so quickly, and yet the push for abortion had been building for several years.

As late as 1967, forty-nine states and the District of Columbia (where there are currently more abortions than live births) classified abortion as a criminal felony. By 1989, a mere twenty-two years later, abortion had become America's most frequently-performed surgery — surpassing appendectomies and tonsillectomies, facelifts and liposuction. Three percent of all women between the ages of 15 and 44 have abortions each year — amounting to one-third of all pregnancies.

In 1967 the New Jersey Supreme Court issued a widely-praised decision protecting handicapped preborns arguing, "We are not talking here about the breeding of cattle. It may be easier or less expensive for the father to have terminated the life of his child, but these alleged deficits cannot stand against the preciousness of a single human life."[1]

As we enter the final decade of the twentieth century, one-half of preborn children with genetic defects are aborted. And Rep. Pat Schroeder (D-Colo.) has expressed outrage that the government should want to require "that absolutely every child should be born, regardless of whether they are wanted, or what condition their parents are in."[2]

A few years ago, geneticist Bentley Class, in a presidential address to the American Association for the Advancement of Science, looked forward to the day when government would require "that no parents will in the future have a right to burden society with a malformed or mentally incompetent child."[3]

How Did *Roe v. Wade* Happen?

This rapid shift in social practice and attitudes is as dramatic as it is unprecedented. Universal criminal prohibition has been transformed into nearly universal legal tolerance in the course of a few decades. The judgment of generations has been overturned within the lifespan of a teenager.

How did it happen? Certainly *Roe v. Wade* was the catalyst. Restrictions on abortion in fifty states were voided at once. The imperial judiciary was in full flower. But the reasoning of the court, as well as the general acceptance of the public, depended on the triumph of two more fundamental contentions.

First, it was argued that laws against abortion were purely modern inventions—ultimately rootless and arbitrary. Justice Harry Blackmun, in *Roe v. Wade,* presented a detailed historical analysis to prove that "restrictive criminal abortion laws are of relatively recent vintage."[4] Laws against abortion were attacked for lack of pedigree.

Second, it was asserted by the court, as well as some medical experts, that anti-abortion laws simply misunderstood the medical facts. Doctors K. Hindell and Madeline Simms summarized the point: "Medically and legally the embryo and fetus are merely parts of the mother's body, and not yet human."[5] Ethicist Philip Wylie was even more blunt, calling the fetus "protoplasmic rubbish" and "a gobbet of meat."[6]

Here one sees the power of words in this debate, which is why it is fitting that "preborn children" and "pro-life" be the words of choice for pro-lifers, not "fetus" and "anti-abortion" as the other side tries to label the babies and their defenders.

In 1973, the court took these historical and medical opinions by people like Wylie, Hindell, and Simms as decisive. But the case was far from proven then. And it has become even more questionable over time.

The Polls: Pro-Abortion or Pro-Life

If the pro-abortionists were not in control of the press, I am convinced that not only would the debate on abortion be over by now (have we really even had a national debate?), but the pro-life side would be victorious because we would have seen the pictures every night on television of what is taking place behind the doors of the abortion clinics and hospitals.

Even with this censorship, when pollsters ask the right question in the right way, they receive answers that the pro-abortion lobby does not want the public to hear.

For example, a March 1988 poll by the *Boston Globe* (which is editorially pro-abortion, making the poll even more credible), found that only 25 percent of Americans favored an unrestricted right to abortion, 19 percent wanted to ban it completely, and 53 percent favored some restrictions. The *Globe* found that huge majorities would ban more than 90 percent of the abortions currently performed. Those include abortions done for emotional strain or inconvenience to the mother.

The figures so often cited by Planned Parenthood, of more than 80 percent who favor abortion in cases of rape and incest and 60 percent who want it for severely deformed fetuses, represent only a tiny percentage of the abortions currently performed.

The *Globe* poll found that legal abortions are opposed by a margin of 89 percent to 6 percent when they are used as birth control, by 75 to 16 when the mother cannot afford to support her child, and by 93 to 3 when the preborn child is the "wrong sex."

Naturally, pro-abortionists are not passing this poll around, preferring to cite their own which often come from twisted questions designed to produce pre-determined answers (i.e., "Do you oppose abortions in ALL circumstances?" or "Would you pass a law which prohibits a woman's right to choose what to do with her own body?").

Historical Sanctions Against Abortion

The legal pedigree of laws against abortion actually goes back to the beginning of law itself. The Babylonian Code of Hammurabi, written in 1728 B.C., contains legal sanctions for intentionally causing a woman to miscarry. Assyrian laws from the twelfth century B.C. impose the death penalty on a woman who causes herself to miscarry, as well as punishments for accessories. Historian Eugene Quay notes that while "the sexual morality of the Hittites was notoriously low," they had prohibitions against abortion that applied to "all persons, means used, and circumstances."[7]

The Roman thinker Soranus spoke against abortion except to save the mother's life. He said, "It is the task of medicine to maintain and save what nature has engendered."[8] The poet Ovid viewed abortion as impious. He wrote, "The first one who thought of detaching from her womb the fetus forming in it deserved to die by her own weapons."[9]

And, of course, the Hippocratic Oath (which most medical schools no longer require graduating students to take), written in Greece in the fifth and fourth centuries B.C., contains the following strong condemnation of abortion: "I will neither give a deadly drug to anyone if asked for it, nor will I make a suggestion to this effect. Similarly, I will not give to a woman an abortive remedy."

The Supreme Court was correct, however, in pointing out that through much of the Middle Ages and the early modern era, the legal protection of nascent life began later than conception. This newer standard, supported by medieval thinkers like Thomas Aquinas and elements of English common law, placed the morally and legally decisive moment for the beginning of life at "quickening" or "ensoulment" — when the child could first be felt in the womb. In general, no legal indictment could occur for aborting a baby before this point. But it was finally a medical discovery that decisively shifted the terms of the debate and created pressure for legal reforms. In 1827 scientists discovered the ovum. Before that point, their understanding of the mechanics of reproduction was vague at best. Now they had the technical ability to pinpoint the beginnings of life. And by the time of the Civil War, an influential anti-abortion movement, often led by doctors and scientists, began to lobby states to revise their statutes in order to prohibit abortion at every stage of gestation.

Justice William Rehnquist, in his dissent from *Roe v. Wade,* noted that by 1868 "there were at least thirty-six laws enacted by state or territorial legislatures limiting abortion."[10] In 1873 the federal government enacted a law entitled, "An Act for the Suppression of Trade in, and Circulation of, Articles of Immoral Use." This legislation prohibited the selling, lending, or giving away of "any article for causing unlawful abortions."[11] By 1910 every state had anti-abortion laws, except Kentucky, whose courts judicially declared abortions to be illegal.

Opinion on abortion, in light of scientific discovery, was nearly unanimous. In 1946 an officer of Planned Parenthood referred to the being produced by fertilization of an ovum as "the new baby which is created at this exact moment."[12] In 1964 a Planned Parenthood pamphlet said, "Abortion kills the life of a baby, once it has begun."[13]

Medical Evidence of Life

It was scientific advance, not scientific ignorance, that led to the prohibition of nearly all abortions for a hundred years. Novelist Walker

Percy, who is also a physician, comments, "The onset of individual life is not a dogma of church, but a fact of science. How much more convenient if we lived in the thirteenth century when no one knew anything about microbiology, and arguments about the onset of life were legitimate. Nowadays, it is not some misguided ecclesiastics who are trying to suppress an embarrassing scientific fact. It is the secular juridical-journalistic establishment."[14]

Medical discovery was the key to the pro-life movement's success in the nineteenth century. But scientific innovation continues to change the context of the debate.

Increasingly, the preborn child is viewed by doctors, not as part of the mother's body, but as a patient. LeRoy Waiters of Georgetown University argues, "It is becoming possible to see the fetus and test the fetus and treat the fetus like a patient, even though it is hidden inside the woman's body."[15] Not long ago, doctors conducted brain surgery six times on a boy, nine weeks before he was born. An ultrasound device had revealed fluid on the brain, and new technology allowed them to drain it. Vitamin deficiencies in preborn children can be detected and treated. Irregular heart rhythms can be corrected. A preborn child can even be given a blood transfusion. This misalignment of science and law began to raise some troubling questions. Legal changes and medical advances have created a situation in which a patient under treatment by a physician can simultaneously lack all legal rights. My colleague, George Will, has commented, "Just as prenatal medicine was beginning to produce marvelous life-saving and life-enhancing achievements, it has become the law of the land that the patients for such medicine have no right to life."[16]

In addition, medical science is increasingly convinced that these tiny patients can not only respond to treatment, but also feel pain. By the fifty-sixth day of a pregnancy, the preborn child can move. It is also possible that movement is caused by discomfort. Stimulation of the mouth produces reflexes on about day 59 or 60. By day 77, the baby is sensitive to touch on its hands, feet, and genital areas and begins to swallow. Professor John Noonan of the University of California Law School contends, "Beginning with the presence of sense receptors and spinal responses, there is much reason to believe that the unborn are as capable of pain as they are capable of sensation."[17]

But medical technology, even as it has clarified the status of preborn life, also cuts the other way.

Sadly, throughout history, medical science and physicians, who have heroically saved lives during plagues and other horrors, have been at the forefront of political efforts to exterminate certain classes of life that an authoritarian elite, answerable to no one but itself, deemed unfit to live. The Third Reich is only the most obvious of these unholy alliances between medicine and government. At least with Hitler we could film the results and hear the testimonies of those who survived. Technology has now brought us to the brink of the ultimate weapon of extermination, and it will be carried out in secret with nothing at all to photograph.

The Abortion Pill: RU 486

In October 1988, the French government ordered a pharmaceutical company to resume production of an abortion pill known as RU 486. Previously the company had withdrawn it under pressure from pro-life groups and the Catholic Church. But France's socialist government ordered the drug back on the market, contending it was "the moral property of women."[18]

The theory behind the abortion pill is simple. When taken early enough, it causes a miscarriage. In essence, RU 486 makes it possible for women to have routine, home abortions as easy as they take an aspirin.

Experiments with the drug are already being conducted in the United States, though it will be several years before it could be approved by the Food and Drug Administration. Pro-life groups have already announced their intention of fighting attempts to legalize this drug in the U.S.

But the drug is already in use in China (where forced abortions are performed) and in Thailand. Many overpopulated Third World countries have made it clear they will be customers. Because it replaces surgery, it can be used by women who don't have access to sophisticated medical care.

And if RU 486 is used that widely, it would be very difficult to prevent the creation of a black market in the United States. Columnist Ellen Goodman comments, "Even if the opposition manages a legal ban, the abortion pill will become available. These pills are called in the trade 'bathtub' drugs; they are easy to make. . . . Anyone who believes that we could control their importation hasn't checked the cocaine business lately."[19]

Faye Wattleton, president of Planned Parenthood, has stated that "the right-to-life movement has seen its last gasp. If these drugs get to the market, the fight is finally all over."[20]

The Present Crisis

The abortion debate is at a critical stage. New science and technology has revealed the unborn child as a "patient," sensitive to pain and under a doctor's care. And this has made it impossible to regard this being as "a gobbet of meat" or even "a part of the woman's body." But, in the future, an abortion could be as close as the medicine cabinet.

And, of course, the legal debate has changed as well. In *Webster v. Reproductive Health Services* (1989), the Supreme Court did not overturn *Roe v. Wade.* But it invited states to again enter the picture and impose new restrictions on abortions. And that has increased activity on both sides of the issue. Political scientist Larry Sabato of the University of Virginia has predicted, "Abortion will become the Beirut of American politics."[21]

As these abstract debates take place, a concrete reality remains. This year 1.5 million abortions will be performed. The United States aborts more babies than any other Western nation. And this casual disposal of life does not come without a price. Dr. Leon Kass, a University of Chicago biologist, says, "We have paid some high prices for the technological conquest of nature, but none so high as seeing nature as mere material for your manipulation, exploitation and transformation. With the [medical science] now gathering, there will be splendid new opportunities for similar degradation of our view of man. Indeed, we are already witnessing the erosion of our idea of man as something splendid or divine, as a creature with freedom and dignity. And clearly, if we come to see ourselves as meat, then meat we shall become."[22]

AT ISSUE

ABORTION

O N E

WHIMSICAL COURT FAILS TO ADDRESS BASIC ISSUE OF ABORTION

D ESPITE THE JOY most pro-lifers feel, the Supreme Court's decision on *Webster v. Reproductive Health Services* appears to be based on nothing more solid than the personal whim of the justices.

Just as *Roe v. Wade* was based on the completely arbitrary "trimester" approach, devised by Justice Harry Blackmun in an attempt to create a synthesis between medical opinion, law, and theology, the court's latest ruling permitting states to restrict abortions smacks of arbitrariness by failing to include an unassailable base for the preborn's right to life that would have provided a standard for the future.

The founders had such a base when they framed the Constitution: "All men are created equal and are endowed by their Creator with certain unalienable rights," among which was the right to life.

The Court makes no reference to any such endowed right for the preborn by a Creator, giving a future court the opportunity to decide what it wishes. One Court giveth; one Court taketh away.

As former Chief Justice Charles Evans Hughes said, "The Constitution is what the Justices say it is," undercutting the foundation of a document that has served us well for more than two hundred years.

The modern court is a product of Justice Oliver Wendell Holmes' dictum, "The life of the law has not been logic; it has been experience." This concept was expanded upon by Justice Felix Frankfurter, who said of the justices, "It is they who speak and not the Constitution."

In a 1958 decision, the court said, "Article VI of the Constitution makes the Constitution the 'supreme Law of the Land.'. . . It is emphatically the province and duty of the judicial department to say what the law is. . . . It follows that the interpretation of the [Constitution] enunciated by this Court. . . is the supreme law of the land."

Such ideas removed the Constitution as the source of the law and replaced it with arbitrary law created by a majority vote of nine justices and what they think about the Constitution at any given moment in history.

Once this view has been allowed to flower, it is not illogical to agree with Donald E. Santarelli, an associate deputy attorney general in the Nixon Administration. Santarelli said,

> [The] Constitution is flexible. . . . Your point of view depends on whether you are winning. The Constitution isn't the real issue in this; it is how you want to run the country and achieve national goals. The language of the Constitution is not an issue. It is what you can interpret it to mean in light of modern needs. In talking about a 'constitutional crisis' we are not grappling with the real needs of running the country but are using the issues for the self-serving purpose of striking a new balance of power. . . . Today, the whole Constitution is up for grabs.

While some pro-lifers can today rejoice that the long national abortion nightmare seems to be ending, they should remember that without a return to law based on an unchanging principle, abortion could again come back to haunt us when a future court, or even this court, decides, for whatever reason, to resurrect *Roe v. Wade.*

For now the court has invited states to pass legislation restricting abortion. And well they might.

The National Abortion Rights Action League estimates that if votes were taken today, only nine state legislatures would decide in favor of abortion on demand. And this is after one of the costliest and biggest advertising and propaganda blitzes in history mounted by pro-abortion groups.

Clearly the momentum has shifted as increasing numbers of Americans became disturbed over unrestricted abortions. As more women testified to post-abortion syndrome and as Operation Rescue made headlines by blocking entrances to abortion clinics, the staggering number of abortions performed daily — four thousand — has become, for many Americans, intolerable.

The Supreme Court has let stand a declaration in Missouri law that "the life of each human being begins at conception." For sixteen years, though, the court concluded arbitrarily that life begins at birth. That decision led to the deaths of more than twenty-four million babies and the emotional scarring of millions of women. Having seized absolute power, the Court did not feel the need to say it is sorry.

Americans should not rest easy, for their Constitution is still in danger of being blown about by shifting legal doctrine and fickle justices.

AT ISSUE

ABORTION

T W O

ABORTION AND THE STATE LEGISLATURES

TAKE OUR RIGHTS; lose your jobs"
is the slogan abortion rights advocates will use against state legislators
who vote to restrict or outlaw abortion on demand.

How seriously should that threat be taken? Not very, if past experience is any indication.

During the ten years the Equal Rights Amendment sought ratification by the states, it was enthusiastically supported by the administrations of Gerald Ford and Jimmy Carter (who personally lobbied members of the Illinois legislature), most of the press, and more than 450 national organizations, from the AFL-CIO to the YWCA and the American Jewish Committee.

It still lost.

Some who now denounce the civil disobedience tactics used by a few in the pro-life movement practiced their own radicalism in favor of ERA. Radical feminists poured pig's blood on the floor of the Illinois State Capitol building and chained themselves to the doors of the State Senate Chamber. They conducted hunger strikes. One ERA proponent was convicted of offering a $1,000 bribe to induce an Illinois legislator to vote for ERA. A Georgia legislator said a pro-ERA woman had offered him her body if he voted yes.

In Florida pro-ERA workers banged on doors of legislators' homes at 7 A.M. to hand them literature. A state senator's driveway was painted with pro-ERA slogans, and the white facade of the state capitol was similarly defaced. The National Women's Political Caucus issued a "dirty dozen" list of state legislators, all male, who "roadblocked the Equal Rights Amendment." According to Stop ERA leader Phyllis Schlafly, none of the targeted dozen lost his next election.

A comparison between ERA supporters and pro-abortionists may be relevant because we are seeing again the same radical tactics.

Following the Supreme Court decision modifying *Roe v. Wade* that invited state legislatures to pass new laws restricting abortion, some opposed to the decision burned American flags.

The real danger for pro-life politicians is that they will likely see waves of television and newspaper coverage favoring the abortion rights people and be inundated with misleading television and radio commercials and newspaper ads which might delude them into believing abortion is favored by a majority of the public.

Rep. James Courter (R-N.J.) played into the hands of radicals when he compromised his pro-life stand in the race for New Jersey governor, apparently hoping to hold on to his support and attract Democratic voters. In fact, such a position is bound to erode his base. Who can respect a politician who takes an expedient position on such an emotional subject as abortion?

If pro-life state legislators want to begin shoring up their positions in advance of the pro-abortion tornadoes that are about to swoop down on them, they might consider the Fourth Congressional District of New Jersey, whose Republican congressman, Chris Smith, has managed to win re-election despite a two-to-one Democratic registration advantage (nearly half his constituents are Independents).

Smith consistently and unapologetically takes a pro-life stand, no matter what opinion polls show. He notes that many of the polls are weighted by the way the question is asked.

Richard Wirthlin's Decision Making Information poll in 1985 asked voters whether they favored "a law prohibiting abortion except in cases of rape, incest or to save the mother's life." Only 30 percent said they would support such a law. Sixty-seven percent wanted to leave abortion as a personal choice.

Smith says he asked the pollster to put the question another way: "Do you believe there should be a law protecting the unborn from abortion on demand?" Forty-six percent said yes, and 45 percent said no.

If pro-life state legislators can withstand the torrent of press propaganda, organized letter campaigns, and a multimillion-dollar ad campaign, the winners will not only be the legislators, but also the babies and their mothers.

AT ISSUE

ABORTION

T H R E E

REPUBLICAN PARTY
FUTURE TIED TO ABORTION

REPUBLICAN NATIONAL Chairman Lee Atwater's timing is a lot better on his blues guitar than it is in politics. Two days before the release of a *New York Times*/CBS survey that shows Republicans near parity with Democrats in party loyalty for the first time in 44 years, and three days before the annual "March for Life" in Washington, observing the 17th anniversary of *Roe v. Wade*, Atwater dropped a bomb on social conservatives who have been the backbone of the party's resurgence.

In a speech to a meeting of the Republican National Committee in Washington, Atwater downplayed the importance of a pro-life position for party candidates when he said, "There is no litmus test on any issue which would be grounds for repudiating a Republican who believes in our overall philosophy and who supports this president and supports this party."

Last November, Atwater was quoted as saying, "I want to make sure that everybody feels comfortable as Republicans, regardless of what their position on abortion is." An unnamed White House official was quoted then as saying that the party "has got to have a message for the '90s, more of a positive vision."

What could be more positive than saving the lives of unborn children and helping women avoid making a mistake so many have lived to regret?

It is difficult to believe Atwater when he says there is no litmus test for Republican candidates. Wasn't previous membership in a racist group a "litmus test" when he, President Bush, and Ronald Reagan campaigned last year against former Ku Klux Klan member David Duke (who subsequently won a seat as a Republican in the Louisiana legislature)? Would Atwater be "comfortable" with Republican candidates who wanted to raise taxes to balance the budget or gut the defense budget and use the "peace dividend" to increase welfare payments? I don't think so.

Perhaps Atwater would say that racism, higher taxes, and a weak defense are not part of the "overall" Republican philosophy. But how can the issue of abortion, which has been as firmly opposed in the last three Republican Party platforms as it has been supported in the platforms of the Democratic Party, not be considered part of the GOP's "overall philosophy?" And what does it say about the integrity of a party that is willing to trade away its biggest moral issue in mistaken hopes of attracting more Republican voters?

There's an exit as well as an entrance to the tent Atwater says he is building for his party. Republicans cannot trivialize the abortion issue and hope to continue to command the loyalty of those social conservatives who have made the party what it is and given it its first chance in more than half a century to claim majority status. Those won over by this new pragmatism will be more than offset by those who will either leave the party, protest by not voting, or support the few pro-life Democratic candidates.

Where does Atwater think this increased loyalty to his party came from? In 1980, the year in which the coalition between social and mainline Republicans was forged, putting Ronald Reagan in the White House and handing control of the Senate to the GOP, only 34 percent of Americans identified themselves as Republicans or leaning toward the Republicans, while 53 percent said they were Democrats or leaning toward the Democrats.

Now the figures are 44 percent Republican and 46 percent Democrat. One does not have to be a professional political analyst to conclude that the party's unswerving stands on social issues such as abortion and "traditional values" have been responsible for its growing strength.

Now that Republicans have won the opportunity to build a party that could set the national agenda and eventually seize control of the Congress, Atwater seems to be saying that Republicans weren't really serious about one of the most critical issues of the last two decades.

Abortion cannot be ignored. As president, George Bush is the head of the Republican Party. If he finds fault with Atwater's thinking and believes the abortion issue is too important to the Republican team to be traded away like an undisclosed future draft choice, he had better say so, and fast. Otherwise that tent the Republicans are building is going to have a lot of empty space inside.

AT ISSUE

ABORTION

F O U R

ABORTING THE MORAL
QUESTION WITH THE BABY

THE AMERICAN MEDICAL Association, at its annual meeting in Honolulu a few days ago, moved one step closer to abandoning the moral argument at the heart of the abortion question.

The AMA's policy-making House of Delegates adopted a statement expanding the organization's official abortion policy: "Early termination of pregnancy is a medical matter between patient and physician, subject to the physician's clinical judgment, the patient's informed consent, and the availability of appropriate facilities."

Said Dr. James Donaldson of Bryn Mawr, Pa., "The appropriate position (on abortion) is no position" for the AMA.

In the abortion debate, moral argument has become the third victim, behind the baby and its reluctant mother.

Yet, as Dr. Leon Kass of the University of Chicago asks in the fall 1989 issue of *Human Life Review,* "Is the profession of medicine ethically neutral? If so, whence shall we derive the moral norms or principles to govern its practices? If not, how are the norms of professional conduct related to the rest of what makes medicine a profession?"

Those who favor the "choice" position wish to operate in a moral vacuum, because to include the moral argument — that is integral in the debate over nuclear arms and wearing fur — is the first step in a long

27

process that will inevitably lead them in another direction—toward valuing life, all life, even that of the unborn. Ralph McInerny, co-publisher of *Crisis* magazine, writes in the December issue, "Anyone who listened to a fair sampling of speeches given to the recent NOW rally will know how morally and logically impoverished is the pro-abortion side. Talk of choice and freedom was drowned out by talk of power. It was clear that most of the speakers could not care less about any moral appraisal of aborting a child. . . . They rally to abortion as to a deed they will do because they can and want to do it. . . . They want power over themselves, over the life of that child, and above all the power to ignore and avoid any discussions of what it is they do. Anyone who talked of picking pockets this way would be recognized as a public menace. They are ideologues and fanatics. But this is quite consistent with their championing an abstract disjunctive freedom."

So it is particularly disturbing when physicians ignore the moral argument in the abortion debate and advocate turning a blind eye toward what is being done. Do they believe that if the morality of abortion is not addressed, the moral question will go away, and they will not be held responsible?

They should heed the advice of another doctor, named Luke, who was not a member of any medical association, but who wrote long ago some sound advice that the AMA ought to consider: "Physician, heal thyself."

AT ISSUE

HOMOSEXUALITY

AIDS AND HOMOSEXUALITY

In 1985 AMERICA'S CONCERN over AIDS was captured by events, channeled by the press, and transformed into panic.

Actor Rock Hudson, after a very private life of homosexual practice, died a very public death from AIDS. Talk of the disease and talk of the most intimate and perverse sexual acts that often produce it moved from medical journals to the cover of *People* magazine. In less than twenty years, we have moved from a medium that would not use the words "toilet paper" to one that openly discusses condoms and various kinds of normal and abnormal sex acts.

The Press Reacts

Newspapers began printing voluminous stories about AIDS, even while the percentage of the population with the disease was very small. Many believe this was because of the presence of large numbers of homosexuals and their sympathizers in the press and entertainment industries.

Of special interest to the press were the relatively few children who were excluded from some schools because they had tested positive for the AIDS virus or, in fact, carried the disease. The attempt was to shift the focus from those who, by their lifestyles, had brought the disease on themselves and on some innocents, to the "intolerant" and "bigoted" people who opposed homosexual sex and intravenous drug use, still the two best ways to get AIDS. The cover of *Life* magazine proclaimed, "Now No One Is Safe From AIDS." *U.S. News and World Report* said that AIDS was now "everyone's disease."

Harvard biologist Stephen Jay Gould warned that AIDS was "potentially the greatest natural tragedy in human history." And he argued, "Yes, AIDS may run through the entire population, and may carry off a quarter or more of us."[1]

Most reputable scientists and immunologists discount such talk now, as it appears that AIDS is remaining for the most part within the high-risk behavior groups with which it has been associated from its inception. The fact is that more than 70 percent of those who have AIDS are homosexuals and most of the rest use drugs intravenously or engage in sex with those who do.

Many in academia and journalism warned of a new era of bigoted intolerance, even violence, toward homosexuals in response to the AIDS "epidemic." One Washington columnist lamented how the disease had "swept away a thin, more liberal, layer of opinion about homosexuality."[2] A magazine reporter wrote, "AIDS is not just a medical story. It is a story about how the straight community is using AIDS to mask their hatred of gays."[3] One homosexual leader in San Francisco warned of a "genocidal" future for homosexuals and compared public health measures against AIDS to the Nazi order requiring homosexuals to wear triangular pink shirt patches.[4]

All across the nation, liberal opinion braced for the anti-homosexual backlash from the AIDS "epidemic." It never came.

Homosexual Political Activism

In fact, something else entirely took place. On March 20, 1986, the New York City Council reversed over twenty years of solid opposition and passed, by a vote of twenty-one to fourteen, a homosexual rights law. Television showed triumphant homosexuals hugging, kissing, and dancing in celebration. They had defied the active opposition of both the Orthodox Jewish community and the Roman Catholic Archdiocese. And their victory, it turns out, was the first of many.

Since 1986 the homosexual rights movement has seen its power grow in cities as diverse as Washington, Miami, and Houston. Los Angeles has passed a bill outlawing discrimination against people with AIDS. New York and San Francisco passed "domestic partnership laws" that allow homosexual (and unmarried heterosexual) couples to register with the city government and be treated—for medical, legal, and inheritance purposes—as married couples.

Thanks to the courageous leadership of Rev. Charles McIlhenny and other concerned San Franciscans, this measure was repealed by the voters in a ballot referendum in November, 1989. Prior to the referendum, McIlhenny and his family were the targets of harassing phone calls and death threats, and their home was peppered with food and paint. Still, they persisted and won. Most of the press view such incidents (repeal, that is) as an aberration and tirelessly pursue the goal of legitimization of the "gay" lifestyle.

The New Republic magazine, a favorite of left-wing intellectuals, ran a cover story in its August 28, 1989 issue titled, "The Case for Gay Marriage," in which the writer, Andrew Sullivan, who is identified as a doctoral candidate in government at Harvard and a "conservative," attempts to make the case for legitimizing homosexual "unions."

The national Democratic Party courts homosexuals just as it does unions and ethnic groups. Ann Lewis, former political director for the Democratic Party (Lewis' brother is Rep. Barney Frank of Massachusetts, an avowed homosexual) put it succinctly: "Gay rights is no longer a debatable issue within the Democratic Party."[5] Nearly every Democratic presidential candidate since 1984 has supported the position that "sexual preference" should be written into the Civil Rights Act of 1964, making gay rights the law of the land. And, during the 1988 New York Democratic primary, all of the remaining candidates for president—Albert Gore, Michael Dukakis, and Jesse Jackson—supported the right of gays to adopt children.

The final goal of this political activism by homosexual rights groups is not simply to end discrimination. In most communities they see very little of that. It is, indeed, to change a social consensus of what constitutes good and evil. *The New York Native,* that city's leading homosexual newspaper, said in 1986, "The gay movement does not exist to elect Mario Cuomo nor even to pass the gay rights bill. These are at best steps in a much larger process, namely, the creation of a genuine acceptance of homosexuality in society at large."[6]

A *Village Voice* columnist was even more blunt: "In the end, the gay alternative means a departure not just from heterosexuality, but from social orthodoxy. . . . In its most moderate politics—the enactment of civil rights legislation—it has radical potential, because civil rights legislation opens the way to dissolution of the norm."[7]

The Homosexual Response to AIDS

Homosexuals might have expected an AIDS-inspired backlash. But just as America discovered this new, deadly disease and identified its source, gay rights groups found a new political momentum. How can this paradox be explained? How is it that AIDS did not impede the efforts of homosexuals to gain legitimacy but, instead, actually seems to have accelerated it?

The answer lies in two influential, and utterly contradictory, arguments forwarded simultaneously by gay rights activists and their supporters.

First, it is asserted that AIDS is not really a homosexual disease; it is "everyone's disease." My colleague, columnist George Will, calls this effort an attempt to "democratize" the plague. Mathilde Krim, founder of the AIDS Medical Foundation, puts it, "Viruses do not discriminate on the basis of sexual preference."[8]

Billboards read, "AIDS doesn't discriminate." One AIDS book designed for distribution to high school students refers to heterosexual sex as a method of transmission while making no reference at all to homosexuality.[9] A sex-education text distributed in Seattle goes even further: "AIDS is not a sexually transmitted disease."[10]

Second, it is argued that AIDS has turned homosexuals into a class of helpless victims deserving special legal protection and treatment. Advocates for gay rights often contend that this disease is just one more instance of "straight" oppression. This type of thinking is consistent with our "no fault" approach to life: no fault accident insurance; no fault divorce. No one is at fault for anything bad that happens. We are all victims.

Charles Ortleg, editor-in-chief of the *New York Native,* claims, for example, that the CIA is to blame for AIDS. He has argued that in 1971 the CIA tried to create economic disorder in Cuba by infecting Cuban pigs with a highly contagious virus. The virus was then transmitted, through Haitians, to the United States.[11]

Other homosexual activists are less conspiratorial, but they similarly place the blame for AIDS on others and call for compassionate activism to help innocent gays plagued by suffering. AIDS patients are painted as the victims of the health establishment that denies them drugs or of the Reagan administration's AIDS panel that, in the words of one columnist, "included several right-wing members out to get the gays."[12]

The Truth About AIDS

Obviously AIDS cannot be the result of a CIA conspiracy *and* a conspiracy of the health establishment and Reagan Administration. It cannot be a non-discriminatory disease that threatens everyone, *as well as* a disease creating a new class of innocent gay victims that deserve our help, money, and respect. These are contradictions. And each of these assertions also fail the test of truth and credibility.

Contrary to what some have claimed (and much of the press promotes), the AIDS virus remains almost entirely confined to the groups in which it began. AIDS is *not* breaking out into the general population. Charles Krauthammer argues, "Indeed, AIDS may be one of the least communicable of all communicable diseases . . . confined to very narrowly defined populations of sexually active homosexual men, intravenous drug abusers, Haitians and hemophiliacs."[13]

The reason is actually quite simple. As a Johns Hopkins University study stated frankly, "In gay men (the overwhelming majority of AIDS patients) 95 percent or more of the infections occur from receptive anal intercourse."[14] AIDS has remained within strict boundaries precisely because it is hard to contract. Michael Fumento comments, "Discussing the sexual transmission of AIDS without mentioning homosexual behavior in general, and anal sex in particular, is like discussing syphilis without mentioning intercourse."[15]

"Every dollar spent," concludes Fumento, "every commercial made, every health warning released, that does not specify promiscuous anal intercourse and needle-sharing as the overwhelming risk factors in the transmission of AIDS is a lie, a waste of funds and energy, and a cruel diversion."[16]

Why then do some seem so anxious to separate AIDS from homosexuality? The reason is as clear as it is dishonest. Fumento recalls, "One San Francisco health official I spoke to, while admitting that AIDS is not now a substantial threat to heterosexuals in that city and will not become one in the foreseeable future, defended the practice of suggesting that heterosexuals were at risk because it made them socially conscious of the problems of homosexuals."[17]

Randy Shilts, the nation's first full-time AIDS journalist at the *San Francisco Chronicle,* stated the ultimate objective even more clearly, "A lot of gay people in AIDS organizations who have spent years watching friends and lovers die are convinced that research money has been slow in coming because AIDS is not seen as a general threat. What has resulted," Shilts argues, "is a concerted effort to create homosexual panic, made by gays, public health officials, and scientists who want research dollars."[18]

And the effort appears to be working. For example, President Bush called for 3.5 billion dollars in federal aid spending in his fiscal 1991 budget, which is more than twice the funding of the previous budget. The nation's number one killer is heart desease (767,000 died in 1989 compared to a cumulative total of 76,030 AIDS deaths since 1981, according to the National Center for Health Statistics), yet, federal money for research and prevention of heart disease in the National Heart, Lung, and Blood Institute budget is only 583,135 dollars out of an overall budget of 1.07 billion dollars. For cancer, the nation's number two killer (488,000 deaths in 1989), only 1.48 billion dollars is allotted to the National Cancer Institute. Stroke, accident, chronic pulmonary disease, pneumonia and the flu, diabetes, suicide, chronic liver disease, and arteriosclerosis round out the top ten killers in America. All receive less money for research, cures, and prevention than AIDS.

So AIDS is not "everyone's disease." But are AIDS patients, admittedly concentrated among homosexuals, just helpless, unfortunate victims? Is Mathilde Krim correct that, "It's just a fluke that AIDS emerged in the gay community?"

Again, the answer is a decisive no. In a Sacramento gay newspaper, two homosexuals with AIDS wrote, "The present epidemic of AIDS among promiscuous urban gay males is occurring because of the unprecedented promiscuity, and the explosion of establishments such as bathhouses, bookstores and back rooms, unique in Western history. It has been mass participation in a lifestyle that has led to the creation of an increasingly disease-polluted pool of sexual partners."[19]

AIDS patients, for the most part, are not a helpless, suffering, and innocent minority. Their disease is not blind in the selection of its victims. It picks those engaged in certain types of dangerous and unnatural behavior, conducted on an unprecedented scale. According to the Center for Disease Control reported that nearly 94 percent of the 122,868 known AIDS cases in America at the end of February 1990 resulted from behavior choices. Only 1 percent of AIDS sufferers were hemophiliacs, only 2 percent received tainted blood transfusions, and 3 percent contracted AIDS from undetermined origins. Dr. Kinsey reported that the *average* homosexual has 1,000 sex partners in a lifetime.[20] The left-wing New York newspaper, *Village Voice*, puts that figure at closer to 1,600.[21] At that rate, and if each partner were equally promiscuous, the size of partners and partners-once-removed comes to a staggering 1,205,604. And one gay activist has asserted that for a "very active" homosexual, 10,000 partners in a lifetime would not be unusual. One study found that more than half of active homosexual males engage in group sex at least once a month.[22]

This is anything but the profile of an innocent victim, set upon by a strange disease of unknown origin that has unfairly and coincidentally singled out two distinct behavior groups (and a few of the truly innocent babies) to be its victims. When homosexuals and their sympathizers deny their role and responsibility for AIDS and seek to shift the blame to others, they ignore a fundamental fact. The disease they fear is rooted in unsanitary sexual practices. It has spread because of intravenous drug use, but its roots remain where they began and no amount of talk or propaganda or misinformation will change that reality.

AIDS is not breaking out into the general population. And the disease itself is mostly caused by anal sex and promiscuity. But this raises one final, key question, asked in an editorial a few years ago by the *Southern Medical Journal*:

"If we act as empirical scientists, can we not see the implications of the data before us? If homosexuality, or even just male homosexuality, is O.K., then why the high prevalence of associated complications both in general and especially with regard to AIDS? Might not these 'complications' be 'consequences'? Might it be that our society's approval of homosexuality is an error and that the unsubtle words of wisdom of the Bible are frightfully correct?"[23]

AT ISSUE

HOMOSEXUALITY

THE POLITICS OF AIDS

THE MISINFORMATION surrounding AIDS and the transformation of language and thought when discussing the world's first political disease has struck fear into the hearts of politicians, journalists, and commentators who are engaged in a silent conspiracy to refrain from saying what needs to be said.

Let me state up front that I, too, am saddened by the deaths from AIDS of more than 75,000 Americans since 1981 and thousands more worldwide. It is a human tragedy, one that requires compassion not only for those who suffer from the disease but also for their families and friends.

Virginia Apuzzo, vice-chairman of the New York State AIDS Advisory Council (a former nun and self-described lesbian), says, "Nothing short of death has been the price that we've paid for growth."

Death has certainly been the price, but growth has not been the result. As Carl Henry notes in his book, *Twilight of a Great Civilization,* "The public argument [about AIDS] shifts the emphasis to undesirable consequences instead of focusing on the root cause: sexual promiscuity and the lack of monogamous relationships."

What Henry sees is "a redefinition of the good life, a redefinition that not only perverts the word 'good' but perverts the term 'life' as well. What is 'good' is corrupted into whatever promotes self-interest even at the expense of the dignity and worth of others. In that fantasy world of sinful desires, shameful lusts and a depraved mind, sexual libertinism is good, coveting and stealing are good, violence and terrorism are good."

This redefinition has trickled down to our public schools and other public agencies. In Oakland, public school teachers are now permitted to discuss discrimination against "sexual minorities" in the classroom.

The American Federation of Teachers voted at its convention in San Francisco to authorize the establishment of a "gay and lesbian union caucus."

In Washington, Mayor Marion Barry asked the city council to consider a bill that would give homosexual couples the same spousal benefits for unpaid medical, birth, or adoption leave as married heterosexual couples.

The Los Angeles City Council voted to extend to unmarried city employees living with a "domestic partner"—whether heterosexual or homosexual—the same sick leave and bereavement leave as members of traditional families.

There are plenty of diseases, including some other venereal diseases, that kill people. A woman with herpes lesions in her birth canal can give the disease to her baby, which can be fatal unless the baby is delivered by Caesarean section. But herpes "victims" are not making headlines. They do not have an effective political lobby. Those who smoke and contract lung cancer or emphysema are not knocking on the doors of Congress, demanding special treatment as a minority or asking for class protection.

The AIDS debate is only partially about AIDS. It is mostly about the legitimization of an abhorrent form of behavior that has been denounced as an "abomination" since Biblical times.

When one thousand demonstrators invaded the Food and Drug Administration offices in Rockville, Maryland, to call for swifter approval of drugs to fight AIDS, they shouted "Shame! Shame! Shame!" It was an appropriate chant, but the shame should not fall on those who labor inside that government office. The shame should cascade down on those who brought this plague on America and who bear the largest part of the responsibility for its continued proliferation.

AT ISSUE

ETHICS

S I X

DRUG WARS FUTILE WITHOUT STANDARDS

THE ANNOUNCEMENT by the Bush Administration of a new offensive in the war on drugs is a necessary first step, but it is only a beginning. Building more prisons to house those who will be swept up in new and expanded drug raids would solve the problem only if there were no other buyers and sellers to replace them. But combatting drugs is like fighting a hydra. Cut off one head, it seems, and two replace it.

At a news conference announcing the Administration's strategy, Attorney General Richard Thornburgh touched on the ultimate solution to the drug problem. He said that only the restoration of "values" in America would break the siege on America's cities.

I agree. The government's renewed emphasis on fighting drugs will fail if it is not accompanied by the restoration of the standards for belief and behavior in our children that the National Education Association once viewed as gospel. The NEA published those standards in 1941 as *The American Citizens Handbook.*

In the book, which it stopped printing in 1968, the NEA detailed its view of what constituted a good citizen and what children ought to be taught to become good citizens.

On page 36 a former college professor wrote of the importance of "intellectual and moral preparedness."

A former Supreme Court chief justice wrote against "self-indulgence, weakness and rapacity." Concerning the origins of the Constitution, the handbook said, "The American concept of democracy in government had its roots in religious belief. This ideal of the brotherhood of man roots down into the fundamentals of religion. The teachings of the Hebrew Prophets and of Jesus Christ inculcate the idea of brotherhood. The growth of the idea gave us the concept of democracy in government. It ennobled home life. It emphasized the sacredness of human personality."

What about "values?" The NEA handbook covered that in a section on "The Code of the Good American:"

> I will control my tongue, and will not allow it to speak mean, vulgar or profane words; I will control my thoughts; I will control my actions; I will try to find out my duty as a good American, and my duty I will do, whether it is easy or hard; I will be honest, in word and in act. I will not lie, sneak, or pretend; I will be loyal to my family, state and country.

Teachers were to be hired who had "moral discrimination," by which was meant that they would "seek to know the right and to live by it."

The movie industry also once reflected and promoted similar standards. For thirty-five years, the Motion Picture Production Code served as a moral guideline for American filmmakers. The code, to which filmmakers were required to adhere, included this paragraph: "No picture shall be produced which will lower the moral standards of those who see it. Hence the sympathy of the audience shall never be thrown to the side of crime, wrongdoing, evil or sin."

How quaint that sounds these days.

The fact is, it will take nothing short of a national assault on "crime, wrongdoing, evil and sin" to reverse the process. But in order for that to occur, a generation must again embrace the standard by which lawfulness, rightdoing, the good, and righteousness are measured.

In pressing for the rights of everyone to live by his own standards, so-called civil libertarians have created a cultural Three Mile Island, whose fallout has infected us all. What has the abandonment of moral and ethical standards produced? For one, a society so wracked by drug violence and abuse that the President declares a national crisis. Unrestrained freedom uninformed by standards has proved to be an empty and dangerous philosophy. The nation should return to what was once a self-evident truth, even to the motion picture industry which, like the educational establishment, saw itself forty years ago as "directly responsible for spiritual or moral progress, for higher types of social life and for much correct thinking."

AT ISSUE

ETHICS

TIME TO REDISCOVER SOME LOST WORDS

T HEN LT. GOV. Douglas Wilder of Virginia said at a 120th birthday celebration for his alma mater, Howard University, that it is time for "a revolution against indolence and sloth." It was refreshing to hear such straightforward use of the language.

"Indolence" has been a part of our language since the seventeenth century, and "sloth" has been around since the twelfth century. And, of course, indolent and slothful people have been with us since the beginning of human history. Yet these words, and many others, have fallen into disuse largely because they carry with them a heavy load of personal responsibility and accountability that might require an admission of guilt and a burden to change one's behavior.

Indolence is a perfectly good word. It means a person who is "averse to activity, effort or movement; habitually lazy." Sloth is also a useful word. It is a synonym for indolence and means, "disinclination to action or labor; spiritual apathy and inactivity." Sloth has a relative in the animal world: "any of several slow moving arboreal edentate mammals that inhabit tropical forests of South and Central America, hang from branches back downward, and feed on leaves, shoots, and fruits." I know people like that.

In recent years these powerful words have been replaced with such watered-down versions as "socially deprived," or, in some cases, "economically disadvantaged." While it is obviously true that a good many people on public assistance are indeed socially deprived or economically disadvantaged, it is also true that some are just plain indolent and slothful. Letting these latter people hide behind euphemisms that cast blame toward society lets them escape the responsibility they have for rising from their lazy behinds and doing some useful work.

"Thief" is another word in danger of disappearing. Those accused and convicted of insider trading on Wall Street, of cheating on their income tax, or of padding their expense accounts view themselves as practitioners of "creative accounting," not as thieves.

Some preachers who consistently overstate the size of their congregations excuse the practice by saying they are "evangelically speaking."

Government officials "misspeak" themselves. Often a better word to describe their pronouncements is "lying," but hardly anyone admits to being a liar anymore.

Few people are referred to as "drunks" or "dope addicts" these days. Instead we say they are "chemically dependent." While the change in language may be appropriate for those who suffer the disease of addiction, it serves as a hiding place for others who turned to alcohol or drugs because they lacked the good old will power to responsibly deal with their problems.

Sex has produced a small glossary of words specially crafted to relieve all sense of guilt and personal responsibility for the way people behave. My favorite story involves a reporter for the defunct *Washington Star* newspaper who interviewed Xavier Hollander, author of *The Happy Hooker*. The reporter asked the admitted prostitute what the difference was between what she did and what her mother used to call a "tramp"?

"Sexual preference" may be the least judgmental words ever created. "Sexually active" are two others. One might inquire of a sexually active person, "what's the difference between being 'sexually active' and what my mother used to call a 'fornicator'?" Fornication is defined as "human sexual intercourse other than between a man and his wife, or sexual intercourse between a spouse and an unmarried person." Isn't this what we mean by "sexually active?" Then why not say so?

We don't say so for the same reason we use "gay" instead of "sodomite," even though we are talking about the same thing: "copulation with a member of the same sex."

Full-page magazine ads for condoms show us a woman who says she would do a lot for love, except die for it. She doesn't mean "love." She means "lust," another perfectly legitimate word that means, "an intense or unbridled sexual desire."

Lieutenant Governor Wilder, who once told members of the Virginia Legislature he would no longer tolerate profanity in his presence during the conduct of state business, is clearly on to something important. He is practicing the highest calling for a word merchant: the use of the right word to fit the right situation.

Using "indolent" and "slothful" to characterize the habitually lazy is a good beginning toward reclamation of the language. Now if progress can be made in resuscitating some of the other words that are on the etymological endangered species list, we might see people taking more responsibility for their own lives and behavior instead of blaming their problems on government, medicine, science, and culture.

AT ISSUE

MORALITY
AND
ACCOUNTABILITY

E I G H T

DIAL *E* FOR EUTHANASIA

N EW YORK — The New Jersey Supreme Court has opened wider the door to a society where euthanasia is fully sanctioned as a way to deal with the problems posed by a seriously ill relative. In its most recent ruling on this matter, the court has now held that a permanently disabled patient's wish to die, or the wish of a surrogate acting on behalf of such a patient, supersedes social standards of "reasonableness and normalcy."

Predictably, within hours of the ruling, families and friends of seriously ill people in the state began telephoning hospitals and nursing homes to see whether they might legally pull the plug on Aunt Bertha or Grandfather Henry in order to lessen the burden on their own lives.

The ruling is not surprising in view of what the courts have already decided concerning preborn and newly-born "handicapped" life. But the bluntness of the court's language shows that one of the few remaining barriers to arbitrary decisions on who should live and who should die is rapidly being dismantled.

Though comatose patients with poor prognoses for recovery are usually considered likely candidates for "plug pulling," the New Jersey court ruling went beyond such cases to include the disabled. In *Jobes v. Lincoln Park Nursing Home,* the court permitted the removal of an intestinal feeding tube from a thirty-five-year-old woman with permanent and profound neurological impairment and held that the nursing home must, despite its conscientious objections, participate in the removal of the feeding device (requested by the patient's husband), which will cause her death.

Edward R. Grant, general counsel for Americans United for Life, said: "This holding forces the hospital to choose between following the law, or following the Hippocratic Oath. . . . (It) thus endangers the rights of doctors and nurses not to act, contrary to their conscience and medical ethics."

In a related case, known as *Matter of Hilda Peter,* the New Jersey court permitted removal of a feeding tube from an elderly, comatose patient. The *Peter* case, like the *Jobes* case, puts the court in the position of allowing, even requiring, the deliberate starvation of a disabled person so long as the patient or his relatives or other designated surrogates approve. If the patient's relatives or other surrogates wish to act out of purely selfish motives and against the wishes of the doctor, it does not matter to the court. If the patient changes his mind after signing over his right to life to a surrogate but is unable to express his new wishes, that's too bad for him. If relatives or friends are tired of giving up part of one day a month to visit the afflicted and want the feeding tube pulled so as not to interfere with Sunday afternoon football, this is their right under the ruling. From here, it is a very short step, indeed, to the killing by more direct means of people who do not measure up to an arbitrary standard for living. Even some of those who have been vocal in their support for abortion and the "letting go" (read starving) of severely handicapped newborns, find it difficult to stomach this ruling. Perhaps they realize that having survived birth and handicaps, they, too, could be a target for extinction by euthanasia.

The New York Daily News had it right when it editorialized against the court ruling: "Maybe a New Jersey man will decide today that his comatose mother would have wanted to be disconnected from her respirator. Maybe tomorrow he'll decide that his comatose mother-in-law OUGHT to be disconnected. The Jersey court has gone far out on a limb. Far out on the slippery slope that leads from the right to die to the right to kill. . . . The court should have stayed out of it. And waited for the elected representatives of the people to do their job."

It is too late for that now. We are already too far down this slippery slope. We have moved from abortion to infanticide to surrogate mothers to surrogate executioners. There can be no turning back until the state

becomes the author of both life and death, or until common sense pre-
vails among the people who will demand that their elected representatives end this judicial tyranny which has led to the courts assuming the
role of God.

AT ISSUE

MORALITY
AND
ACCOUNTABILITY

GOOD GOLLY, MS. MOLLY

P RESIDENT BUSH wants to send as-
tronauts to Mars, but Molly Yard and her band of angry spitfires seem
to be already there.

Yard and her legion held more of a wake than a convention in Cin-
cinnati a few days ago. The National Organization for Women's annual
"mad" revealed symptoms that can be diagnosed as the feminist
movement's death rattle. In desperation, born of their failure to enact
their radical agenda, the sixteen hundred delegates voted in favor of a
constitutional guarantee for abortion on demand, voted to promote "lesbian rights," called for "gender balance" laws requiring that 50 percent
of appointments to all government boards and commissions be women,
and requested that NOW's leaders explore creation of an independent
political party.

When any group threatens to form a third party, you know it is just
a matter of time before it folds its tents and departs the scene.

In a last-ditch effort to advance its moribund agenda, NOW—like an
old-fashioned spinster—is also attempting a marriage of political conve-
nience with environmentalists. Of course, if NOW really represented the
majority, it wouldn't need a coalition.

Former NOW President Eleanor Smeal told the delegates that the
public might dub some of the convention's resolutions as "stupid,"
"naive," and "weird," but it was only through provocative proposals that

women would achieve full equality. She was half right. The ideas *are* stupid, naive, and weird, but they have nothing at all to do with equality.

Feminism has never been about equality. It has been an ideology with its own radical political agenda. From drafting women for combat; to the sexual integration of the Boy Scouts, Girl Scouts, and 4-H Clubs; to "gender neutralizing" the language so that hurricanes (him-acanes?) are named for men as well as women; to using the all-purpose "Ms." before a woman's name without asking her whether she wishes to be so designated — this band of ideological migrants has yet to find a home in the mainstream of American political and family life.

Just how far these feminists have gone into space can be observed in the classifieds of *Ms.* magazine. There are numerous ads appealing to homosexuals, including "lesbian pen pals," religious cults, and a book claiming to reveal "136-plus Biblical Contradictions."

This is mainstream America? I don't think so.

Some feminists are now acknowledging that NOW went too far and the backlash is about to do them in.

The Washington Post's Judy Mann wrote a column titled "NOW's Flirtation With Suicide" in which she criticized suggestions of a third-party movement. At the same time, the Democratic Party, that embraced so many elements of NOW's agenda, has lost the White House for so many elections that it might wish radical feminists *would* form their own party. Like many movements that are fueled more by anger than common sense, the radical feminists can't keep from cannibalizing themselves philosophically.

Feminist writer Germaine Greer wrote in her 1970 book, *The Female Eunuch*, "If women are to effect a significant amelioration in their condition, it seems obvious that they must refuse to marry." Greer called for women to be "deliberately promiscuous," but not conceive babies.

By 1984, Greer had done an about face. In *Sex and Destiny,* she launched an "attack upon the ideology of sexual freedom" and blamed artificial birth control for the decline of fertility in the West, decried the breakup of the family and sex for its own sake, criticized the 600,000 annual sterilizations in the U.S., and said the exportation of contraceptive technology to the Third World is "evil."

As Dinesh D'Souza has written in *Policy Review,* "Susan Brownmiller, whose *Against Our Will* alerted an entire generation of feminists to rape and sexual politics, now scarcely misses an opportunity to excoriate the women's movement. It ignores 'profound biological and psychological differences' between men and women, she says, and is fixated on issues . . . which she finds 'dumb' and 'dopey.'"

The NOW convention made the usual threats to lobby the White House, but if I were George Bush, I wouldn't lose any sleep. They didn't vote him in. It's not likely he can do anything that will satisfy them. As more Americans tire of their shrillness, radical feminists will become less and less visible, like Mars on a cloudy night.

AT ISSUE

MORALITY AND ACCOUNTABILITY

BABY BOOMERS GO BUST

F ROM THE START, they were a generation to which much was given, from which much was expected. Born in the decades following the end of World War II, they were brought up to feel that they were the chosen generation—something new and promising under the sun. They were, literally, the future for which the war had been fought."

So begins the second part of a survey of the baby boom generation conducted for *Rolling Stone* magazine by Peter D. Hart Research Associates. Part one exposed the generation's shocking lack of commitment to country by revealing that 40 percent of this privileged class could not think of a single circumstance under which they would fight to defend America. Part two documents the reason for this lack of national commitment. Guess what? The boomers are preoccupied with themselves.

Yes, the generation that was going to bring peace on earth, that would end racism and sexism, that rolled in on the waves of the Age of Aquarius ("harmony and understanding; sympathy and trust abounding," remember?) has overdosed on more than drugs and "free love." It has also overdosed on self-deception. For while the survey reports that 61 percent of the boomers say they are quite or extremely satisfied with their lives, "the data suggests otherwise."

David Sheff, who wrote the survey's summary, says, "Their avowed optimism, in the face of their specific concerns, resembles a refrain from the Randy Newman song, 'My Life Is Good,' in which the protagonist cheerfully ignores all evidence to the contrary."

The boomers were raised with unprecedented choices, but without the powers of discrimination to make the right choices. A comment by one respondent pretty well sums up their dilemma: "My parents believe in doing what you are told to do. I believe you should be able to do what you want to do."

Says Sheff, "Doing what they wanted to do turned out to be more thorny than the idea of being able to do what they wanted to do. They may have been far less restricted by society's codes of morality, but in the absence of these, they were also completely unprepared for what they encountered."

"I don't think we're emotionally equipped to live with so many options," said one woman who participated in the survey. "There's just too much freedom," said another respondent. A woman in her early thirties is quoted as saying, "Everyone my age that I know is going sort of crazy."

This spoiled generation seems dissatisfied with everything.

Having rejected the concept of traditional marriage in favor of "alternate lifestyles," when they did marry, half their marriages ended in divorce.

Less than half reported a high degree of satisfaction with their jobs, and less than a third expressed satisfaction with their financial condition.

The generation that rejected materialism and condemned their parents for contributing to poverty by embracing capitalism rather than socialism now says money is its top concern, followed closely by the desire to stay healthy.

Asked how they would spend an extra hour in the day if they were granted one, "not a single person said he or she would spend the hour on community service or political work."

"Do as I say, not as I did," seems to be the only moral authority this generation can summon to persuade their own children to resist the drugs they tried and the sex they had in abundance, which they now regret. Somehow, "just say 'no'" doesn't have much impact coming from a disciple of Timothy Leary.

The *Rolling Stone* survey sums up the desperation of this generation in a concluding sentence: "Perhaps one statistic implies their acknowledgment that something in their thinking is unresolved: The members of this generation, unlike their predecessors, embrace psychiatry as something to be relied on."

On July 5, 1926, President Calvin Coolidge delivered a speech to mark the 150th anniversary of the Declaration of Independence. In it he said, "A spring will cease to flow if its source be dried up; a tree will wither if its roots be destroyed. . . . We cannot continue to enjoy the result if we neglect and abandon the cause."

Maybe that is why spring has yet to arrive for the baby boomers, and why they are still trapped in the winter of their own discontent. In abandoning self-control in favor of no control, they have uprooted their lives as no generation before. Now their lives have withered and they are desperately searching for nourishment. For them, as C. S. Lewis wrote, "it is always winter, but never Christmas."

AT ISSUE

MORALITY AND ACCOUNTABILITY

ELEVEN

THE ROOT CAUSE

O N ABC'S "THIS WEEK," Manhattan Borough President (now Mayor) David Dinkins said finding the "root cause" must be our primary goal in the case of the gang of young boys who went on a rampage in Central Park, randomly attacking people and beating and raping a young woman, leaving her near death.

During the police interrogation, one of those arrested referred to the woman he allegedly raped this way: "She was nothing."

Nothing? What is the "root cause" of that statement? Where did such an idea come from? Certainly it did not come from the ideas celebrated in New York during the observance of the bicentennial of George Washington's inauguration. Washington and his colleagues believed people had been "endowed by their Creator with certain inalienable rights."

Yet to one young person the now comatose woman was "nothing" and thus fair prey for a roving band of buzzards to swoop down on and pick apart.

I predict the real root cause of this gang violence will be found in the magazines these boys have read, the television they have watched, the movies they have attended, and the music they have heard.

Serial killer Ted Bundy told the nation he murdered women because he was "addicted" to pornography. Some dismissed Bundy's confession as another of his con games. But the evidence is increasingly on Bundy's side. Look at the images that now form our regular entertainment diet. It is nearly impossible to get through a day without being exposed to an act of sex or violence or a combination of the two. From soap operas, to prime time TV, to the movies, to MTV, come the message that our fellow human beings are, as one of these young boys viewed the New York woman, "nothing."

At a 1984 Symposium on Media Violence and Pornography, sponsored by the Ontario Institute for Studies in Education, fifty panelists critiqued the modern menu of sex and violence that is available to anyone who wants it (and many who don't want it).

Among the material considered was an *R*-rated film called *The Tool Box Murders,* which began with an erotic scene of a beautiful young woman taking a bath. In the next scene, a stocking-faced intruder enters her house and mows her down with tracer bullets.

The rock group Kansas has a video called "Fight Fire With Fire," which depicts a nude woman surrounded with flames. Other music videos are far more graphic.

A battery of researchers reported at the Canadian symposium that in the field of violent/pornographic movies, prolonged exposure to *X*-rated as well as *R*-rated films caused male college students to be "desensitized" to rape and violence and more accepting of the rape-myth that women say no when they really mean yes. Neil Malamuthy, a psychologist and sexual violence researcher at UCLA, reported at the symposium that "otherwise normal men" exhibited attitudes "similar to convicted rapists," and about a third said there was "some likelihood" that they would rape a woman if they thought they could get away with it.

The National Institutes of Mental Health reported in 1982 that "television violence is as strongly correlated with aggressive behavior as any behavioral variable that has been measured." The "cult murders" in Matamoros, Mexico, were tied to a film which depicted Satanic activity.

Here is the root cause for "wilding" — as they call the spree of violence committed in Central Park — and related antisocial behavior: There are more adult bookstores (between fifteen and twenty thousand) than there are McDonald's restaurants; there are 350 child pornography magazines published in America; 500,000 calls a day come into "dial-a-porn" numbers in New York City alone; every week, at five hundred "adult" theaters, Americans buy two million tickets to *X*-rated movies, leading to $500 billion a year in revenue; an estimated one-fifth of all videocassette sales are *X*-rated movies; bestiality cassettes are sold over the counter in New York City; direct mail sales of pornographic material are now at $3 billion annually; a computerized sex service, SEXTEX, offers an "electronic orgy" to anyone with a computer. Add to this the "everyday" fare of increasingly violent broadcast and cable TV and you have societal poison. So why is it shocking when someone concludes that a New York woman is "nothing" after he has been surrounded by such pollution? Those who refuse to acknowledge a connection between bad images and undesirable behavior must reconsider. The correlation is becoming overwhelming. Until the "root cause" is dealt with—the proliferation of filth in our society—we can expect more incidents of violence like the tragedy in Central Park.

AT ISSUE

MORALITY AND ACCOUNTABILITY

T W E L V E

THE "DECENCY DECADE"

THERE ARE THOSE who like to label decades, and people have been wondering what to call the 1990s. *Good Housekeeping* magazine editors have decided they want the next 10 years to be known as the "Decency Decade." No one can quibble with that.

However, the magazine also has been trying to sell a very interesting label of its own: "New Traditionalist." The magazine has an ad campaign featuring pictures of "new traditionalist" women and their daughters. There are no husbands or fathers in these pictures. The magazine's editor, John Mack Carter, tells me this was a marketing decision designed to reflect the readers of the magazine and not a surrender to the single-family household as the societal norm.

In an ad, which ran full page in *The New York Times, Good Housekeeping* summarizes the findings of a new study it commissioned by "marketing futurist Faith Popcorn of Brain Reserve."

The study says, "It will be a very good decade for the family as traditional values become the strong, moral foundation for a more caring, more decent America." But read on and discover what the magazine considers "traditional values": "better day care, better health care, better housing, better education, maternity leave, flex time, and advancement opportunities for working mothers . . ."

What happened to the tradition of mothers caring for their families at home? Carter says the magazine has not abandoned the "older" traditional values, but that these "new" traditional values are merely a reflection of the concerns of the baby boom generation.

I don't know. To me it sounds as if the magazine, inadvertently or not, is promoting the same tired liberal litany to be found in the last several Democratic Party platforms. The cost for this "new traditionalism" must be underwritten by someone, and numerous special interest groups want the federal government to pick up the tab.

Still, in an oblique way, *Good Housekeeping* may be on to something, just as Tevye was when he sang "Tradition" in "Fiddler on the Roof." As Republicans grope for a bankable campaign theme after the demise of the "Red menace," they should consider the unfinished agenda on the home front, which begins with the dilapidated condition of the American family and the need to re-establish traditions that have a proven track record.

If a "peace dividend" accrues from the lessening of world tensions, let it first go in the form of tax breaks to families with young children so that women who wish to stay home with their children in the important early years will not feel pressured to work to make ends meet.

Then, how about a campaign against teen-age sex? The liberals claim that all teen-agers can't wait to have sex, and that they'll have it no matter what, so let's teach them how to avoid getting pregnant and contracting a venereal disease. No teen-ager is ready for the emotional consequences of sex. Period. The current "sex education" in the schools is a form of spiritual and political molestation.

As Gary Bauer, president of the Family Research Council in Washington, notes, "something must be done about the sex merchants in this country, including Republican businessmen who use sex to sell everything from toiletries to cars to beer." Is there any politician brave enough to address this issue and withstand the cries of "censorship"?

Welfare, which has virtually destroyed the unity once enjoyed by poor families and left so many fatherless, must be reformed. Welfare is a social drug that has been as addictive as the other kind.

No-fault divorce, 20 years old this year, has been a disaster, throwing millions of women and children into poverty. While it may have made easier the parting of husbands and wives from their mutual and uncoerced pledge to stay together, it has hit the nuclear family with the force of a social atomic bomb, the fallout from which will continue to be felt for generations to come.

Real traditions — such as devotion to family, hard work, responsible behavior, intellectual and spiritual development — built and sustained this nation. Traditions became traditions because they worked. They proved themselves, and they were accepted by most Americans. Laws were written that supported these traditions because leaders realized they were essential in promoting the general welfare. The *Good Housekeeping* ad concludes with this: "America is looking for something to believe in." America *had* something in which it once believed, but we abandoned it in favor of self-serving values that have produced so much misery. Let us hope that our country will not go the way of other empires that first collapsed from within before being conquered from without.

Republicans are uniquely suited to pick up this mantle of real tradition if they do not falter in the face of strong liberal rhetoric and media manipulation.

The political leader who puts liberals on the defensive because of what they have unleashed on America for the past 30 years can win the support of the substantial number of Americans who are tired of three decades of indecency and would welcome a decade of real decency.

That kind of decency isn't going to be achieved by bulging day-care centers funded by tax dollars. It will be had when the real traditions of America are resurrected, and we rediscover that what we used to believe is worth believing again.

AT ISSUE

THE CHRISTIAN FAITH

THIRTEEN

JUSTICE O'CONNOR'S "CHRISTIAN NATION" LETTER

W HEN A FELLOW Arizonan wrote to Justice Sandra Day O'Connor concerning Supreme Court cases that alluded to America as a "Christian nation," O'Connor's response — though rather innocuous — generated a firestorm of controversy. Her letter listed three such cases — from 1892, 1952, and 1961 — that are often cited by those who want to emphasize how far this country has drifted from its moorings.

O'Connor's correspondent then used the letter in a political debate in Arizona which resulted in the passage of a resolution by the Arizona Republican Party proclaiming this country as a "Christian nation."

Those who have been working overtime to censor the history textbooks and erase our memory banks so that no student will discover this country's religious roots, and the rest of us will forget them, went ballistic.

So-called "legal experts," such as Harvard Law School Prof. Laurence Tribe, said that by answering her mail, Justice O'Connor had entered a debate that was "potentially politically charged," and that she should have known her response "could obviously be misused."

The otherwise conservative court watcher Bruce Fein said the letter was "grossly improper" and "borders on the inexcusable."

Definitions are important in this case. If what is meant by "Christian nation" is that Christian or Biblical values are currently reflected in the culture, then this is decidedly not a Christian nation.

If, however, the term is meant to suggest that the nation was founded on principles which were drawn from the laws and moral requirements in the Old and New Testaments, then there is ample historical evidence for such a claim. And, properly understood, those ideas provide the greatest amount of freedom for all, even for those who are not Christian in their faith, within a framework of "promoting the general welfare" and insuring "domestic tranquility."

Apparently Tribe believes the law was invented in the twentieth century. But back when Harvard law students (and students at virtually every other law school in America) read William Blackstone's *Commentaries on the Laws of England,* published between 1765 and 1770, it was clear from where our laws and ideas for social order came.

Historian Daniel Boorstin found Blackstone's *Commentaries* so influential that he wrote, "In the first century of American independence, the 'Commentaries' were not merely an approach to the study of the law; for most lawyers they constituted all there was of law."

Some examples from Blackstone rebut the objections of Tribe and Fein: "The doctrines thus delivered we call the revealed or divine law, and they are to be found only in the holy scriptures. Upon these two foundations, the law of nature and the law of revelation, depend all human laws; that is to say, no human laws should be suffered to contradict these."

For Blackstone, it was obvious that the source of all laws was God, whether they were found in the Bible or in nature. Said he, "Man, considered as a creature, must necessarily be subject to the laws of his Creator, for he is entirely a dependent being. . . . And, consequently, as man depends absolutely upon his Maker for everything, it is necessary that he should in all points conform to his Maker's will."

Drawing on such a concept of man inspired Thomas Jefferson to write of "certain inalienable rights" that are "endowed by our Creator." If Jefferson were alive today and said such things, he would be attacked by the ACLU and Laurence Tribe for violating the Constitution he helped to frame.

Tribe should read the graduation address of Harvard President Joseph Willard, who urged the class of 1799 not to reject "the sacred code called the Bible in which you have been instructed from your early years and which is worthy of all acceptation, and that none of the writings of infidels have unhinged your minds or removed from them the hope of the gospel."

Willard then linked this "sacred code" to one's public life and to the nation: "And while you are reaping the greatest advantages for yourselves, you will be heartily disposed, whether as members or heads of families, private citizens, professional men, or politicians and public officers, to promote in the community, to the best of your ability, the interests of pure religion and good morals without the prevalence of which there can be no lasting prosperity and happiness in any nation."

Given this and much more history, Justice O'Connor is on solid ground in providing facts to her correspondent, and her critics are on sinking sand.

AT ISSUE

THE CHRISTIAN FAITH

FOURTEEN

RELIGIOUS HYPOCRISY CUTS BOTH WAYS

Now THAT THE SEX, money, and power scandals involving certain television evangelists seem to have played themselves out, it is time to look at behavior on the religious left. Though not as titillating, questionable actions by the left may be far more widespread and hypocritical in scope.

The rather unlikely person to expose the so-called "mainline" denominations is Roy Howard Beck, bureau chief for Booth Newspapers, a small chain that is part of the Newhouse newspapers organization. For six years Beck was employed by the *United Methodist Reporter,* the world's largest religious newspaper.

Beck could win a Clark Kent look-alike contest, and underneath his bespectacled, mild-mannered exterior is the tenacity of a Superman, dedicated to holding the mainline churches in America to the same standards he has used to assess the religious right.

In a book titled *On Thin Ice,* Beck documents a group of churches that not only have a radical left agenda, but also employ half-truths, deception, and intellectual dishonesty in pursuit of their goals.

His revelations are those of an insider who took extensive notes and whose veracity is, therefore, difficult to challenge.

For example, at a 1981 conference on ways to end apartheid in South Africa, funded by the United Methodist Church, Beck soon discovered that the conference's steering committee was pursuing a greater objective: "I had fairly certain identification of more than half the steering committee. Besides the staff members from the United Methodist Women's Division, the rest were identified with the U.S. Peace Council, the U.S. Communist Party, ANC (African National Congress, a black nationalist group active in South Africa), SWAPO (the Marxist South-West African People's Organization), the International Association of Democratic Lawyers, and groups identified by themselves or by the U.S. government as affiliates of the lawyers' 'Soviet Front Group.'"

Beck writes of a conversation he had with Nora Boots, head of the United Methodist Mission Board's Latin American section: "As I took my first bite of a BLT sandwich, Nora took a bite into my profession. 'There's nothing particularly free about the press in the United States,' she said. 'The press is much freer in Cuba.' Nora had a way of offering ideas for people to choke on. . . ."

Of particular concern to Beck was the strong tilt of mainline churches toward criticism of right-wing dictatorships while seeming to accept the human rights problems in countries ruled by left-wing totalitarian regimes. He found the National Council of Churches had four complaints against regimes of the right for every one against a leftist government.

Beck says the mainline churches, which saw themselves as not only the keepers of the religious flame, but also the conscience for social justice, have ceased to be an effective voice "because they've lost their moral spine. They now lack moral and intellectual integrity when they speak on social issues." We also learned from Beck that the religious left is not as tolerant as it portrays itself: "I found that once the word 'racism' got attached to any endeavor, person, organization, or line of thinking, rational discussion usually was ended. Just as people sometimes can shut off discussion by accusing a person of being a Marxist, the same effect was ensured by labeling people as racist, sexist, homophobic, McCarthyite, and a number of other epithets."

And, like the conservatives whose motives and tactics he once criticized, Beck found that the religious left doesn't like to be held accountable: "For the first time in my life, I was covering an institution dogmatically liberal in its leadership. And I was finding that liberal power figures squeak the same way that conservative power figures do when their deeds are held up for public observation."

The religious left has had its fun during the past year as it watched the scandalous behavior of some on the religious right. Roy Beck's book shows that there is an even bigger beam in the eyes of the membership of the National Council of Churches. It is a timely and needed contribution to a decade of dynamic religious activity in America.

AT ISSUE

THE CHRISTIAN FAITH

FIFTEEN

THE RETIRING BUT NOT SHY JERRY FALWELL

THE RESIGNATION of Jerry Falwell as president of Moral Majority means that "leftists," "militant homosexuals," and "secular humanists," as the fund-raising appeals read, won't have their favorite bogeyman to kick around anymore. In fact, Falwell's resignation may do more to put some of his adversaries out of business than anything he did during his eight years as head of one of the most controversial organizations of modern times. You can't raise money without a threat — and Falwell was a gold mine for the left.

Falwell brought fundamentalists and conservative evangelicals out of the closet with a vengeance. He made their creed respectable, confronting Phil Donahue and Ted Koppel with disarming ease and charm. Some hated his agenda, but few who knew him could dislike the man. In this way he mirrored his hero, Ronald Reagan.

When the Moral Majority became a household word in 1980, only a year after its founding and at a time when I was serving as its chief spokesman, it sought to fill a vacuum created by the perceived incompetence of Jimmy Carter and a moral crisis created by years of encroaching secularism. But the opportunity to transform the culture was quickly squandered when it was decided to emphasize fund raising instead of building the political machinery necessary to exercise real power.

Many of the organization's state chapters were little more than a name and a telephone number, the national office having decided to keep the money. Liberals, at first intimidated by what they believed to be an unstoppable hoard of Ayatollah-like fanatics, soon emerged from hiding to confront what turned out to be a paper tiger. For all of the media attention, the Moral Majority never saw even one of its major social goals enacted. It did not stop abortion or restore school prayer, two of its declared reasons for being.

Though Falwell has turned the presidency of the organization over to an Atlanta businessman, it cannot prosper without his charismatic presence. Its income has been dwindling. The Moral Majority is now little more than a fund-raising machine and probably will be forced to shut its doors for all practical purposes after the 1988 election.

Falwell's presence on the national scene produced positives and negatives, for the country and for the image of the Christian church.

On the positive side, no one will be able to run for public office in the foreseeable future without taking into consideration the views and values of the conservative religious community. If that was all Falwell achieved, it would be enough to earn him a place in the history books.

Of even greater and longer-lasting significance has been Falwell's example that has re-introduced many fundamentalists to intellectual pursuits. He founded an accredited university. He wrote books. He debated at Harvard, Yale, Princeton, and Oxford. He confronted what former Alabama Gov. George Wallace called "pointy-headed liberals" on their own turf and won. He was (and is) a master at television, the cultural icon. No one ever beat him in a TV debate, not even Rev. Jesse Jackson.

Yet there was a dark side to this force. Liberals worried that religious involvement in political matters threatened the Constitution. In fact, the greater danger was to the evangelical church and its message. The constant need for money to feed the television piranha—which spawned those outrageous claims in some of the fund-raising letters—eclipsed the central theme of the gospel: that life was to be found in Christ, not in the Republican Party. The ridicule heaped on Oral Roberts following his "death threat from God" and the scandals involving Jim and Tammy Bakker were the predictable results of a movement that had gotten its priorities seriously out of order.

As one who worked from 1980 to 1985 with Falwell, during the halcyon days of the Moral Majority, I saw both the pluses and minuses of politically organizing conservative Christians. The biggest minus is that those who proclaim a Power higher than Caesar will make the state their primary focus of worship, a form of idolatry. Unable to persuade by the Spirit, many attempt to take a short cut to success through more secular means. The effect is to dull the primary spiritual power of the Church and transform it into another special interest group with which politicians must deal.

Indeed, a top assistant to Vice-president George Bush was widely quoted as having said that all you have to do to get the fundamentalist vote is "go to their meetings and quote a few Bible verses."

But the downsides to religious involvement in politics do not mean there should be abstinence. They merely require a warning that priorities must not get out of line. When Republicans or Democrats, liberals or conservatives, are viewed by religious believers as the salvation of the republic and its citizens, then troubles develop. There has been, should be, and always will be a tension between "the kingdoms of this world and the kingdoms of our God." When the lines become blurred, problems for one or both can result.

AT ISSUE

ENTERTAINMENT

THE MOVIES

THE MOVIES HAVE BEEN a source
of moral controversy from the beginning. In 1896, outrage greeted one
of the earliest one-reelers. An article in the family periodical, *Chapbook,*
exclaimed:

> In a recent play called *The Widow Jones,* you may recall a famous kiss
> which Miss May Irwin bestowed on a certain John C. Rise and visa
> versa. Neither participant is physically attractive, and the spectacle of
> their prolonged posturing on each other's lips was hard to bear. When
> only life-size, it was pronounced beastly. Magnified to gargantuan pro-
> portions and repeated three times over, it is absolutely disgusting. . . .
> The Irwin Kiss is no more than a lyric of the stockyards. Such things
> call for police interference.

Films quickly got much worse than May Irwin's rather chaste kiss,
and the opposition of religious groups escalated with every actor's leer-
ing glance and every inch of raised hemline. The history of the film
industry is, in large part, the history of an American public demanding
from its entertainment both moral uplift and immoral titillation. Since
America has never had a federal censor, that basic conflict of expecta-
tions has traditionally determined what is morally permissible on
Hollywood's back lots. And, in the past, it was a fairly even fight.

The Twenties: Roaring

In the 1920s, spicy and suggestive filmmaking had the upper hand. Many new films reflected the moral relativism and materialism of the decade. Lust was a much-explored vice in the cinema of the Roaring Twenties. Married couples had extramarital flirtations. Film heroes became urbane, wealthy, and immoral. The new wealthy and materialistic audience, spending as much as two dollars to get into posh movie houses, enjoyed what they were seeing. It was true that the movie industry had its own National Board of Censorship, but it was simply ignored and, therefore, irrelevant.

The increasing immorality on the screen in the 1920s was accompanied by a string of scandals off the screen. "America's Sweetheart," Mary Pickford, got a Nevada divorce and married Douglas Fairbanks just three weeks later. Fatty Arbuckle was charged with manslaughter concerning the mysterious death, with sexual overtones, of a young girl at one of his parties. Leading man Wallace Reid died suddenly, generating a scandal when the press discovered he was a drug abuser.

This kind of notoriety brought the United States Congress to the brink of federal censorship—the last thing a producer or director would want. In desperation, rather than out of conviction, the frightened movie industry decided to clean its own house before it was cleaned for them. In 1922, film producers selected Will H. Hays as president of the Motion Picture Producers and Distributors of America and charged him with improving the image of the industry. Hays was President Warren Harding's campaign manager, a Presbyterian elder, and a Republican. The Hays office, as it came to be called, did not act as a censor. It countered Hollywood's bad publicity, regularized business practices, and encouraged producers to voluntarily submit their films for pre-release examination.

The Thirties and Forties: Decency

Over time, however, it became clear this was not enough. The willingness of the movie industry to ignore its own censorship code in pursuit of greater profits finally drove American Roman Catholics into action.

Cardinal Dougherty of Philadelphia owned a home across the street from a huge billboard which advertised the latest movies, often with lurid pictures. One day, in 1933, Cardinal Dougherty was incensed by a particularly tasteless advertisement. The next Sunday, he declared all movies in Philadelphia off limits to every Roman Catholic under his authority.

In April 1934, the Roman Catholic Church convened a committee of bishops, forming the Legion of Decency. Parishioners across the country were instructed at their Sunday Mass to recite an oath not to patronize any movie condemned by the church. An "A" could be seen in good conscience, but a "C" was condemned as an occasion for serious sin. In its first year of operation, the Legion threatened a nationwide economic boycott at the same time the movie industry began feeling the effects of the Great Depression.

The unsettling prospects of millions of unsold movie tickets forced the industry to act. A new censorship code was adopted in June of 1934, and this time the industry also created powerful machinery to enforce it. A new Production Code Administration within the Hays office, headed by a Catholic layman named Joseph Breen, would grant a seal of approval to films that observed a strict set of moral restraints. Any producer who released a film without the seal would be fined $25,000.

The intention of the new code was clearly outlined: "No picture shall be produced which will lower the moral standards of those who see it. Hence the sympathy of the audience should never be thrown to the side of crime, wrongdoing, evil or sin." The code specified that films were to avoid brutality or sexual promiscuity. It contained specific prohibitions against a number of objectionable words, including, along with the usual suspects, "tart," "goose," "madam," "pansy," and "nuts." It forbade the criticism of any religious group, required proper treatment of the American flag, and outlined appropriate standards for modest costumes and dance movements. All the sex in Hollywood ended up on the cutting floor. "That may sound uncomfortable," said Fred Allen, "but that's Hollywood."

The Breen Code was viewed by many producers and directors as oppressive. But during the years it was in effect, Hollywood experienced its golden age, producing some of its most acclaimed and popular classics. Changes required by the code were sometimes silly, but seldom drastic. The code forbade moviemakers from showing the techniques of murder in any detail, evidently to keep people from using movies as a "how to" manual. So the word "arsenic" was struck from many scripts. Electrocutions were forbidden, so the opening scene was cut from *Double Indemnity*. Showing childbirth was off limits, so Scarlett and Melanie were forced into silhouette in *Gone with the Wind*. Mention of prostitution was condemned, so Donna Reed was turned into a bar girl in *From Here to Eternity*. Married couples were invariably placed in twin beds.

The Fifties and Sixties: Decline

It was finally the advent of television that changed the rules of moviemaking and put new pressures on the code. In 1956, Sam Goldwyn noted sourly, "Why should people go out and pay to see bad movies when they can stay home and see bad television for nothing?" This new form of competition, according to observers at the time, threatened the existence of the movie industry. Movies, many producers felt, had only one advantage. One film critic has commented, "Because television applied even stricter moral regulations to its programs than the 1934 Breen Code did to films, film producers could lure audiences to the theater with promises of franker, racier, 'more adult' entertainment."[1]

Many films were, in fact, adapted novels. It was impossible to make movies like *Peyton Place, Lolita, Butterfield 8,* and *From Here to Eternity* without dealing with issues such as adultery, fornication, and homosexuality—all topics that would attract viewers from the more sedate fare of television. And viewers were receptive. One critic noted, "Ironically, the Code, which Hollywood adopted for business reasons in 1934, perished some thirty years later for the same reasons. The very words and deeds that crimped sales in the 1930s, spurred them in the 1950s."[2]

The battle of the movie industry against the code began in 1953 with Otto Preminger's deliberate decision to release *The Moon Is Blue* without the code's seal of approval. Preminger reaped a commercial and publicity bonanza. Two years earlier, in 1951, the stage had been set by the Supreme Court which decided, for the first time, that movies were part of America's "press" and so were entitled to constitutional protection under the First Amendment.

From 1953 to 1968, the strict moral principles of the code were forced to bend as the movie industry looked for a lure that television lacked. Year after year the Production Code Administration hedged and became more inconsistent. Exceptions were made for prestige films like *Lolita, Alfie,* and *Who's Afraid of Virginia Woolf?* Finally, in 1968, the old system was scrapped. A new rating board was created to measure the "level of maturity" of the film, rather than prohibiting certain types of material—the system of *G, PG, R,* and *X* we now use. *PG-13* was added in the 1980s after much debate within the industry in response to growing criticism that too many *PG* rated movies were beginning to resemble *R* movies in incidents of sex, language, and violence.

The Seventies and Eighties: Sex and Violence

Almost immediately, with the removal of all effective restraints, Hollywood's rules for moral permissibility shifted. In the summer of 1970 one of the nation's largest studios, Twentieth Century Fox, released two new films. The first was *Myra Breckenridge,* an explicit story of transvestitism and homosexual rape. The second film was *Beyond the Valley of the Dolls,* a big-budget work of explicit pornography that concludes with a decapitation, a sword-stabbing, and two women gunned down, one by way of a pistol fired into her mouth.

This new reality of post-code Hollywood is characterized by two dramatic changes. First, and most obviously, movies use increasing doses of sex and violence to increase their box office income. Today's films commonly offer scenes of voyeurism, adultery, incest, prostitution, homosexuality, and rape—usually without any moral context. And second, producers, directors, and actors increasingly view movies as a tool of progressive political education and change.

Taking this second point first, Richard Grenier has argued, "The cinema is becoming an increasingly ideological medium."[3] And no wonder. Film critic David Brooks observes, "Screenwriters are uniformly on the left side of the spectrum. Among actors, directors, producers and so on, the community is about 70 to 85 percent liberal."[4] "Most of the 'bankable' stars of Hollywood these days," says Grenier, "are liberal Democrats."[5]

Actor Tom Selleck, speaking from the inside of the industry, says, "There is a cultural war within the business [between movie executives and movie creators]. Yet both groups are predominantly liberal."[6] When a recent Hollywood writers' strike was at a point of critical and heated disagreement, a producer from Lorimar Studios is reported to have told a group of writers, "We can get together and work this out. It's not like any of us are Republicans."[7]

The bias of Hollywood is more than the action of a few, well-placed individuals. It seems rooted in its institutions. David Prindle, in a book on the Screen Actors Guild, found that among those who went to acting school, 70 percent consider themselves politically progressive. Among those who did not, 67 percent consider themselves conservatives. And this uniformity of opinion constitutes a definite worldview.[8] "It is here," Ben Stein once said, "that serious, intelligent people believe that the world is run by a consortium of former Nazis and the executives of multinational corporations."[9]

The results are evident in their product. Businessmen are invariably painted as evil. Religious leaders are stereotypes of corruption. Moral conservatives are intolerant hypocrites. And the American government always seems to side with oppression. Richard Grenier writes of viewing two recent movies. The first, titled *Daniel,* praises Julius and Ethel Rosenberg—committed Communists convicted of supplying nuclear secrets to the Soviet Union in the 1950s. The second, titled *Under Fire,* praises journalists as heroes for deliberately falsifying news from Nicaragua to bring American aid to the Sandinistas. "Exporting anti-American movies," Grenier concludes, "is a real Hollywood growth industry."[10]

But overtly political movies are often box office failures. *Daniel* and *Under Fire* were flops. The most palpable public damage does not come from politicization but from an advanced state of moral decay—the first effect of a loss of moral standards at the movies.

Theologian James Wall comments, "Forty years ago, when a fourteen-year-old boy read an illegal copy of D. H. Lawrence's *Lady Chatterly's Lover,* he was exposed to explicit sexual descriptions. But that was nothing compared to the sex and violence his grandson sees today when he views in his home a cassette of a film like *I Spit On Your Grave.* "It is obvious," Wall concludes, "that the entertainment industry's pursuit of profit is overruling its good taste and civic responsibility."[11]

Those who produce these images, whether in print or on film (but especially on film) argue that there is no connection between such images and human behavior. Why, then, do advertisers spend millions of dollars on television commercials which seek to persuade us to buy a certain brand of soap, tires, cars, and beer? And what about the "in case of fire, walk, don't run, to the nearest exit" advisory on the movie screen? Is this not about producing a response by the audience in case the theater catches fire?

If there is a connection between images and the sale of a commercial product, why is there not a connection between an idea or a simulated action and similar behavior by at least some of those who view it? The answer is that there is such a connection and claims to the contrary by the movie industry are false.

The most disturbing aspect of the immorality of many recent movies is what Edward Donnerstein of the University of Wisconsin calls "the eroticization of violence."[12] Slasher films like *The Tool Box Murders* and *Friday the 13th* make money by stressing a linkage between violence and sexuality, a combination also found in more respectable films. Testing a sample of eighteen- to twenty-two-year-old males, Donnerstein found a dramatic difference in their reaction to film clips focusing separately on erotic material, on violent material, and on a combination of the two. The last category of erotic violence was by far the most effective in changing attitudes. In follow-up research, he found that after this exposure, the subjects were more tolerant of rapists and more skeptical of the testimony of rape victims when they viewed mock jury rape trials. Donnerstein concluded his subjects had been "desensitized."[13]

Pamela Hansford Johnson says, "Only a minority of people act out what they have seen. But I believe a great number become desensitized by being exposed to scenes of, or ideas of, violence. I have seen the young become increasingly unshocked by the screened or staged display of cruelty. What would it be like if they met with the real thing? Such as Hitler's public humiliation of the Jews? Crowds excitedly gathered round old Jewish victims in Vienna. They were laughing. Are we preparing ourselves for a good laugh?"[14]

This process of desensitization to sex, violence, and especially a combination of the two, proceeds in a downward spiral of increasing velocity. Images soon lose the power to shock and must be replaced in an unending race with boredom. As G. K. Chesterton commented, "Men seek stronger sins or more startling obscenities as stimulants to their jaded sense. . . . They try to stab their nerves to life, as if it were with knives of the priest of Baal. They are walking in their sleep and try to wake themselves up with nightmares."[15]

The consequences are serious, not only to individual virtue, but also to social order. "What if," asks George Will, "contrary to Freud and much conventional wisdom, shame is natural to man and shamelessness is acquired? If so, the acquisition of shamelessness through the shedding of 'hangups' is an important political event. There is a connection between self-restraint and shame. An individual incapable of shame and embarrassment is probably incapable of the governance of self. A public incapable of shame and embarrassment about public vulgarity is unsuited to self-government."[16]

AT ISSUE

ENTERTAINMENT

AND THE LOSERS ARE . . . THE MOVIEGOERS

W HILE HOLLYWOOD indulged in its annual self-congratulatory awards ceremony, outside and virtually ignored was a coalition of Vietnam veterans, Vietnamese natives and students who charged that the winner for Best Picture, *Platoon,* is a dishonest portrayal of the war. If the atrocities depicted in the film are based on true events, then producer Oliver Stone is guilty of withholding information on war crimes.

Stone has said the film is "loosely" based on his combat experiences in Vietnam. Charles Wiley, executive director of the National Committee for Responsible Patriotism, countered that the film plays loose with the truth by depicting U.S. soldiers as murderers, rapists, racists, and drug users.

Said Veterans of Foreign Wars member Ken Thompson, "Even if Stone is on a guilt trip over his own past, he has no right to create a film that blackens the reputation of all those who served our country with honor and dignity in Vietnam."

What disturbs me, after watching *Platoon* and other war films that make strong political statements, such as Stone's *Salvador,* an earlier and, thankfully, unsuccessful attempt at countering U.S. policy in Central America, is that those who make films for the giant screen and the smaller television variety want us to view them as artists when, in fact, they are often propagandists for their own political and moral world views. At least with the Soviet filmmakers, some of whom recently visited Hollywood to compare notes with American colleagues, one is never in doubt as to their primary purpose: to influence the minds of the masses to the government's way of thinking.

It is not only political statements that some in Hollywood feel compelled to make. A few days before the Academy Awards ceremony, the Alliance for Gay and Lesbian Artists held its sixth annual awards show in Los Angeles. The awards honor the "responsible portrayal" [read that "the way we want to be portrayed"] of homosexual characters on screen, television, and in theater. Phil Donahue — who frequently appears to be doing penance for being born a man, an American, a married heterosexual, and a baptized Catholic — stripped away the thin veil of creativity that masks the ugly face of propagandist when he told the audience that he intended to continue bringing gay issues to his viewers so they can understand that "sexual preference or habits is *nobody* else's business" (emphasis his). Unfortunately, AIDS has made it *everybody's* business (emphasis mine).

Business is another easy target for Hollywood. In spite of their own business success, Hollywood writers and producers often portray business people as evil and corrupt. On a PBS program, "Hollywood's Favorite Heavy: Businessmen on Prime Time TV," narrator Eli Wallach noted that businessmen on television "seem to make an awful lot of money, without ever having to work hard or produce useful products. To succeed, all they seem to do is lie, steal, cheat, blackmail, even murder." It is the absence of counterweights in films about the Vietnam war, Central America, homosexuals, and business people that has transformed Hollywood from the entertainment capital of the world to the propaganda capital. Fortunately, a few, like Columbia Pictures' David Puttnam (*Chariots of Fire, The Mission*), still make movies the old-fashioned way, primarily to entertain. Now playing at some movie theaters is a film called *The Hanoi Hilton.* It's not likely to win any Academy Awards (name the last anti-Communist film that did), because it attempts to show life as it really was inside a North Vietnamese prison camp.

Maybe some theater owner will revive a long-lost theater tradition and show *Platoon* and *The Hanoi Hilton* as a double feature — and maybe they'll drop the price of a ticket to a quarter again.

AT ISSUE

ENTERTAINMENT

NBC CENSORS ITS "CENSOR"

THE NATIONAL Broadcasting Company is eliminating its broadcast standards department, which had reviewed every program and commercial for possibly objectionable material before it aired.

Under the new system dreamed up by NBC's owner, the General Electric Company (whose slogan during Ronald Reagan's tenure as their chief TV spokesman was "progress is our most important product"), the producers of the programs to be aired on NBC will now decide the boundaries of good taste. (No Hollywood producer has ever been indicted for having good taste, so will NBC tell them where to find it?)

NBC President Robert C. Wright says the broadcast standards office will be converted into a new department that will try to make shows more commercially profitable, such as finding product tie-ins. This would allow advertisers, among other things, to promote their products using characters from the programs they sponsor.

In the not-so-distant "old days" of television, all three networks had large broadcast standards departments. Their function was to examine every program for violations of good taste. They would even scrutinize commercials to make sure advertisers' claims were valid.

Why would networks want to abandon this socially responsible task? Well, audiences have been shrinking, not only because of the diversity of programs offered by cable, but also because of the declining quality of programs aired. In NBC's case, the transformation of the censor's office into a promotion arm of the network is supposed to help shore up a declining audience and keep commercial rates at current levels.

Entertainer Steve Allen, who created and hosted the "Tonight" show on NBC between 1953 and 1957, is uncomfortable with the concept of censorship, but he tells me that in certain situations "abuses become so flagrant that the abusers themselves bring on the very sorts of controls about which they later complain."

Allen, a genuine talent who never had to rely on crude humor, recently sent a letter of protest to the head of a major commercial network after witnessing on a comedy program "an allegedly comic routine about flatulence. To make the subject matter and its development even more objectionable, the physical setting for the sketch was a restaurant. You don't have to be as saintly as Mother Teresa to regard that sort of juvenile vulgarity as objectionable."

All three networks (CBS and ABC are headed toward the elimination of their broadcast standards departments, too) have been engaged in fulfilling their own prophecies. They have conditioned us to accept low-quality shows, and then they say that because fewer people are watching they must serve up even lower quality shows to appeal, not to the head or the heart, but to baser instincts. If the networks continue their downward quality slide, they may preserve for themselves a small share of television's audience, but they will be trading their reputations for short-term financial gain.

PART TWO

ISSUES FRATERNAL

★ ★ ★

AMERICA
AND ITS GOVERNMENT

AT ISSUE

FREEDOM AND DEMOCRACY

THE MAKING
AND UNMAKING
OF DOMESTIC POLICY

S OME PEOPLE THINK this is the most powerful office on earth, but I will frequently give an order, only to see it frustrated several levels down in the bureaucracy."

Ronald Reagan said that to me as we had lunch together in the White House in 1986. Later, Reagan would blame what he called the "iron triangle"—made up of the press, liberal special interest groups, and academia—for controlling much of the policy agenda that presidents in times past have set.

How is government policy made (and unmade)? Open any high school textbook on American government and you will discover the process that the founders laid out for an orderly implementation of policy and laws in a system of carefully delineated and divided powers. The Congress makes the laws. The President enforces them. The courts interpret them.

It is a model that recalls the distant memory of the Constitutional Convention in the steamy summer of 1787, when the founders closed the doors to debate and drafted a system of government that was elegant in its design and constructed for durability over the long haul. It is a view that presupposes careful deliberation by principled and disinterested men and women in dignified and solemn assembly. It recalls the integrity of individuals like John Tyler of Virginia, who wrote in 1818:

> I have thus briefly, Fellow Citizens, presented you the reasons which have governed me in the course which I have pursued upon these subjects of greatest importance to our future destiny. Should I have been so fortunate as to have coincided with you in opinion, it will be to me a source of gratification. . . . But should my course not meet with your approbation, I have the consolation to know that I have honestly pursued the dictates of my best judgment, and acted the part of an independent Representative.

This is the American government of textbooks. Memorize the system, and the teacher will give you an "A" in that course. Attempt to implement that system in the real world of domestic American politics in the 1990s, and you will fail miserably because the model no longer resembles the reality.

The Federal government has changed so dramatically from its original design that it would be unrecognizable to those who created it. Reporter Hendrick Smith comments, "When I came to Washington in 1962, I thought I understood how Washington worked. I knew the textbook precepts . . . but these old truisms have been changed dramatically. I have watched a stunning transformation in the way the American system of government operates."[1]

America has seen the development of a new set of rules when it comes to exercising power to shape public policy. And those rules place much of the real influence outside the official structures of American government. The traditional branches of executive, legislative, and judicial have been changed, even overshadowed, by the branches of a new political order: media, pressure groups, and academia. These three elements form an alliance for activism that is more powerful and more effective than the three branches of government.

Policy by the Press

When Harry Truman ordered the atomic bombing of Hiroshima and Nagasaki in 1945, he announced his decision to the entire White House press corps — 25 reporters. By 1987, about 1,700 men and women held

regular White House press passes. In 1961 there were only 1,500 journalists accredited to the Congressional press galleries. Today that figure
stands at 5,250. All told, there are currently an incredible 12,600 journalists based in Washington, D.C.

That numerical increase has been matched by an increase in influence. "One correspondent with one cameraman," David Halberstam has
written, "can become as important as twenty senators."[2] Many journalists can identify with Halberstam's recollection of his motivation for entering journalism: "I believed deeply that journalism had a crucial role
as the societal conscience of last resort."[3]

Once, reporting "facts" was enough for the American journalist.
Now, in the wake of Watergate and Vietnam, journalists feel a calling of
almost divine magnitude (though few believe in the divine) to shape and
even direct events according to their own worldview of what is best for
America and the planet. Journalists (and all of the media) are the new
aristocracy, the inheritors of the ancient "divine right of kings" in which
the monarch was the final and unchallenged authority on how things
must and ought to be.

This shift in power and influence in the formulation and direction of
domestic policy has occurred because of the almost singular worldview
of the press and entertainment industries. Fewer than twenty percent of
American journalists have ever supported any Republican candidate. In
the 1989 race for Governor of Virginia, CBS *60 Minutes* reporter Ed
Bradley and PBS' Charlayne Hunter-Gault donated hundreds of dollars
to the Democrat candidate, Douglas Wilder, in what was clearly a conflict of interest and a breach of journalistic ethics. Neither was disciplined, though the policy of both networks clearly prohibits direct political involvement by reporters.

During a 1989 pro-abortion demonstration in Washington, D.C.,
several reporters and editors for *The Washington Post,* as well as the
Supreme Court correspondent for *The New York Times,* marched in soli-
darity with the protestors.

Yet, even with this evidence of crusading bias, the press largely sets
the agenda for social change. Gallup president Andrew Kohut writes,
"We believe and value what journalists tell us, even while we also believe they can be rude, biased, subject of outside influence, and prone to
other sins as well."[4] Robert Lichter argues, "To a degree that was hardly

envisaged a generation ago, the major media stand at the center of the struggle for social influence. They act as gatekeepers for the messages contending groups and individuals wish to send to each other and to the general public."[5]

Policy by Special Interest Groups

The second group to weigh in the new American balance of power are aggressive pressure groups. In 1961 there were 365 lobbyists registered with the Congress. Today, there are over 23,000. That amounts to 43 special interest lobbyists for each of the 535 members of the House and Senate.

Though this explosive growth of public interest organizations can be found on both the Left and the Right, they have served the interests of the Left with extraordinary effectiveness. Arch Puddington has argued, "The contemporary Left's job has been simplified by the absence of serious left-wing parties whose ideologies, programs, or foreign links might elicit public scrutiny and hostility. Instead of working through organized parties, the Left presses its agenda through single-issue projects. . . . At any given time, it has going literally hundreds of project coalitions, committees, task forces, and commissions of inquiry. Many achieve little beyond the very complexion of American politics."[6]

The leadership of these groups is remarkably homogeneous, even in comparison to the press. Robert Lichter, in a study of leaders and top staffers in seventy-four public interest organizations such as the ACLU, Common Cause, Public Citizen, and the Consumers Union, concluded, "The liberalism of public interest leaders shades into profound dissatisfaction with the American social and economic order. . . . In fact, their alienation was one of our most striking findings. Three out of four believe the very structure of our society causes alienation, and over 90 percent say our legal system favors the wealthy. . . . Only about half the public interest leaders believe the system can be salvaged. . . . Ninety-six percent of the public interest elite voted for George McGovern in the 1972 election."[7]

Policy by Academia

The third player in this new ideological version of a Monopoly power game is a politicized academia. A Columbia University English professor has written, "What has changed most since 1968 has been the faculty, especially the junior faculty. They are the children of the sixties. They were marching then, but now the political action takes place in the classrooms and in scholarly books dedicated to social change."[8]

As events in Europe at the close of 1989 swept away four decades of entrenched communism, it now appears that the only people who still believe in the principles of Marxism-Leninism are in American universities.

Harold Taylor argues, "Many of the students involved in the reform movements in the early and middle 1960s have gone on to graduate schools with no slackening in their enthusiasm for the causes with which they were identified as undergraduates. Their social views, especially on questions of race and poverty, are radical, and at the same time are becoming politically respectable."[9]

This is the intellectual home of liberal political activism. According to Balch and London, the Left is "comfortably ensconced within a network of journals and professional organizations, university departments, and academic programs. [They are] distinguished by the view that scholarship and teaching are preeminently, and unavoidably, extensions of politics."[10]

A Shared Worldview

These three groups — the press, pressure groups, and liberal academia — work in ideological tandem and are extraordinarily effective in achieving their common goals. They are effective, not because there is a conspiracy hatched in the basement of some secret society, but rather because theirs is a set of shared attitudes and objectives. The outcome is similar to that of a conspiracy without the danger of exposure that a true conspiracy might bring.

In fact, membership in each of these groups is porous and, often, interchangeable. Academia provides policy experts to be "talking heads" on news programs. Congressional and executive staff become journalists and the other way around. Academics join pressure groups or write for publications. These shared connections and convictions amount, in the end, to a singular worldview or ideology. Alexander Bickel has described this view as

> the abandonment of reason, of standards, of measure, the loss of balance and judgment. Among its symptoms were the incivility and even violence of rhetoric and action that academics and other intellectuals domesticated into their universe of discourse. . . . Our recent revolutionists have offered us hatred. They despise and dehumanize the persons, and they condemn the concerns and the aspirations, of the vast majority of their countrymen. They have offered for the future, so far as their spokesmen have been able to make clear, the Maypole dance and, in considerable tension if not contradiction, a vision of "liberated" masses abjuring profit, competition, personal achievement, and any other form of gratification not instantly and equally available to all.[11]

A United Goal: Bork

The effectiveness of this new alliance found its most dramatic expression in the fight over the nomination of Robert Bork to the United States Supreme Court. Concerning that event, *Time* magazine observed, "All at once the political passion of three decades seemed to converge on a single empty chair."[12] The Bork nomination brought the full force of the "iron triangle" to bear on a matter of profound social, legal, and political importance.

Senator Ted Kennedy fired the opening salvo before hearings had been scheduled. In an effort to buy time while the liberal organs planned their strategy, Kennedy took to the Senate floor and launched a scurrilous attack on "Robert Bork's America" in which he accused Bork of wanting to return the nation to the days of slavery and of women tied to the kitchen and bedroom. That the speech lacked any substantive facts was of little interest to the press, which reported it as if it had been well documented and researched and accurately reflected Judge Bork's opinions.

As Bork recounts in his book, the Senate Judiciary Committee, with four of the Senate's most liberal members (Kennedy of Massachusetts, Alan Cranston of California, Howard Metzenbaum of Ohio, and Chairman Joseph Biden of Delaware), decided to postpone its confirmation hearings, allowing seventy-seven days to elapse before hearings began. The average time between nomination and hearings had been fourteen days, but the Left had much to do and needed the time to do it.

"Kennedy hired Anthony Podesta, the founding president of People for the American Way, whom the *Globe* identified as a liberal lobbyist, to work on organizing opposition," writes Bork.[13]

The pressure groups leaped into the fray. "According to the *Globe*," writes Bork, "'Kennedy woke up Rev. Joseph Lowery at the Hyatt Hotel in New Orleans before the Southern Christian Leadership Conference's annual convention.' As a result, 'Lowery turned the entire day's meeting into an anti-Bork strategy session. From that meeting, the issue made its way into black churches throughout America.'"[14]

Forty-five liberal civil rights organizations held a strategy session at the Washington office of the Leadership Conference on Civil Rights, an ultra-left group that served as one of the stalking horses against Bork's confirmation.

People for the American Way, founded by Hollywood producer Norman Lear, sent out a mailing to editorial writers at 1,700 newspapers. PAW also ran a series of radio ads in Washington and print advertisements in newspapers around the country attacking Bork and misrepresenting his judicial record. Most news organizations, particularly the networks and the most influential newspapers, reported these attacks with little, if any, attempt at correcting the misstatements and distortions of fact.

Perhaps the most scurrilous misinformation campaign of all was conducted by the American Civil Liberties Union. As Judge Bork recounts, the ACLU sent out a "Western Union priority letter. . . . It contained statements in full capitals such as: 'DETAILED RESEARCH REVEALS BORK FAR MORE DANGEROUS THAN PREVIOUSLY BELIEVED. . . . WE RISK NOTHING SHORT OF WRECKING THE ENTIRE BILL OF RIGHTS. . . . HIS CONFIRMATION WOULD THREATEN OUR SYSTEM OF GOVERNMENT. . . . TIME IS SHORT. . . . URGE YOU TO RUSH EMERGENCY CONTRIBUTION AT ONCE.'"[15] Legal academics were trotted out to raise questions about Judge Bork's fitness for the Supreme Court, though there had been no opposition to his confirmation for other court and governmental posts in which he had served.

All of this opposition influenced the press to carry negative stories about Bork which were, according to some who kept score, more than two-to-one negative. In one three-month period, television featured eighty-six people critical of Bork and only sixteen who spoke favorably of the judge.

The battle over Bork was the most blatant example since the days of Watergate and the Vietnam War of the unholy alliance between leftists in academia, the press and entertainment industries, and special interest groups. In an information age, the philosophy that dominates the airwaves strongly influences the policy that is ultimately adopted, regardless of whether elected leaders originally believed that policy to be best for the country.

Something important was lost in the Bork battle. Saul Bellow observed, "The heat of the dispute between Left and Right has grown so fierce in the last decade that the habits of civilized discourse have suffered a scorching."[16] The civility and deliberation essential to democracy seems worn and tattered. Our public life threatens to become, in the words of Henry Adams, "politics as the systematic organization of hatreds."[17] It is not likely to get better. The Left has a well-honed strategy and a philosophy to which it is fanatically committed. It knows that it cannot persuade the American people to accept that philosophy (if they did, they would have voted liberals into the White House in recent elections), and so it transcends institutions by campaigning through the organs it owns and runs.

This is why Ronald Reagan was so often frustrated, and it is why George Bush and any future president whose philosophy is not liberal can expect the same treatment. Unless this troika of press, academia, and special interest groups is broken up, the Left will effectively control the direction of policy into the next century, no matter who is in the White House.

AT ISSUE

FREEDOM
AND
DEMOCRACY

THE AMERICAN REPUBLIC: CAN WE KEEP IT?

T EN SCORE YEARS AGO, our forefathers ratified a Constitution for the newly independent United States of America. In 1787, freedom not only had a purpose and a meaning, it also had a price.

The freedom our founders sought was not a means for pursuing self-indulgence but a tool that could, as stated in the Preamble to the Constitution, "insure domestic Tranquility, promote the general Welfare, and secure the Blessings of Liberty to ourselves and our Posterity."

Often, it has been a visitor from a foreign land who has reminded us of the fragile privileges we enjoy and how tenuously we cling to them. de Tocqueville was one. Solzhenitsyn is another. Now comes Pope John Paul II.

In Columbia, S.C., the Pope warned against the continued breakdown of the family. He blamed the breakdown on "a false notion of individual freedom" and warned Americans to use their freedom wisely.

"It could be a great tragedy for the entire human family," said the Pope, "if the United States, which prides itself on its consecration to freedom, were to lose sight of the true meaning of that noble word. America, you cannot insist on the right to choose, without also insisting on the right to choose well, the duty to choose the truth." The Pope also said the breakdown had occurred because "fundamental values, essential to the well-being of individuals, families, and the entire nation, are being emptied of their real content."

He is right. Freedom, emptied of its real content, more closely fits the meaning of *license*: "freedom that allows or is used with irresponsibility; disregard for rules of personal conduct; licentiousness."

The late Bishop Fulton J. Sheen spoke of freedom's limits in 1979: "Rights are related to personal dignity and identity. . . . But how do we know the identity of anything? By its limits. How do I know the identity of a football field? By its boundaries. How do I know my identity? By my duties, my responsibilities—and they are principally to God, to neighbor, to my country. . . ."

Our founders recognized such duties, which must be assumed with a deep sense of responsibility. Fifty-six of them signed the Declaration of Independence, but not all survived to see the Constitution's ratification. All paid a price for their commitment to obtain freedom for the common good.

Nine died in the Revolutionary War. Five were captured by the British and died under torture. Twelve had their homes ransacked and burned to the ground. Dr. John Witherspoon's home and college library were burned. Thomas Keen was forced to move five times in as many months to escape capture. He settled at last in a log cabin on the Susquehanna. Thomas Nelson, Jr., when his home was occupied by British Gen. Charles Cornwallis, urged Gen. George Washington to open fire and destroy his house. He died in poverty.

The fifty-six had pledged their lives, their honor, and their liberty. Seventeen of the signers lost everything they had. Many lost their lives, all of them lost their liberty for a time, but none lost his honor. It was because they knew the meaning and purpose of freedom.

Today, "freedom" seems to mean the right to abort one's child or to censor certain lofty ideas from the public schools while tolerating the filthiest of pornography as First Amendment-protected speech and press. Conviction in political leaders is seen as "extremism." It is thought better to consult the polls to arrive at a bottom-line consensus than to posit firm standards of right and wrong and challenge the nation to follow. Had the founders behaved similarly, the Queen of England would be pictured on our money.

The United States was founded and the Constitution written on the basis of certain universally held presuppositions. Because those presup-

positions are under attack and words like "freedom" have been, in the Pope's words, emptied of their real content, the future is less certain than perhaps at any time since our beginning.

We would do well to recall Benjamin Franklin's response to the woman who asked him what kind of government the founders had produced. "A republic, madam, if you can keep it." Keeping it, so far, has been our greatest achievement. Keeping it for our posterity will be our most formidable challenge.

AT ISSUE

FREEDOM
AND
DEMOCRACY

NINETEEN

WHAT YOU DON'T KNOW CAN PUT FREEDOMS IN DANGER

A HEARST CORPORATION survey has found that in this bicentennial year of the Constitution, most of the country does not understand the meaning of the document. The survey of 1,004 Americans revealed that only a bare majority knew that the purpose of the Constitution was to create a federal government and define its powers; that 59 percent were unaware that the Bill of Rights is the first ten amendments to the Constitution; and that nearly half believed the Constitution contains the Marxist declaration, "From each according to his ability, to each according to his need."

Large majorities incorrectly ascribed certain powers to the President, such as to unilaterally declare war and to appoint justices to the Supreme Court without Senate confirmation.

Hearst Corporation President Frank A. Bennack, Jr. said the survey showed him that "Americans today have a confused understanding of the Constitution's basic tenets and provisions."

Constitutional attorney John Whitehead, president of the Rutherford Institute, an organization that argues First Amendment cases, believes that knowledge of the Constitution is critical to maintaining its integrity and guaranteeing that the freedoms we now enjoy will be passed on to future generations.

"Without a working knowledge of the founding document which preserves basic rights and freedoms," notes Whitehead, "how will citizens appeal to that document to protect them when those rights and freedoms are challenged?" The Hearst survey suggests that public opinion polls can be misleading because they tell us nothing of how a person formed his or her opinion. The late philosopher-theologian Dr. Francis Schaeffer once said that most people catch their presuppositions the way they catch a cold. They don't know how they acquired the germ or opinion; it simply showed up and infected them.

This point was illustrated by Charles Colson, the Watergate figure, who told me that upon his conversion to Christianity, he immediately sought out "my favorite Bible verse, 'God helps those who help themselves'"—in vain. "It has to be in the Bible," he said. "I've heard it all my life." The admonition is not in the Bible, and the fact that Colson had heard it all his life and believed it Biblical did not make it so.

Lack of knowledge about common cold germs and the Bible may not cause long-term harm, but ignorance about our fundamental freedoms could place us in jeopardy. On more than one college campus, students have told me that some forms of expression violate the First Amendment "mandate" separating church and state. When I point out that such language is not in the First Amendment but in court rulings since 1947 which have used the phrase and caused it to have the force of constitutional law, they rarely have a rebuttal. When I ask them to quote the First Amendment, most have been unable to do so. As with Colson, truth in their minds has been formed by repetition, not investigation. Clearly there is a relationship among knowledge, opinion, and action, but there is also a link among ignorance, opinion, and action.

This relationship between knowledge and opinion was for seven decades behind the Soviet government's denial of access to its people of information about the world that differed from the party line, because it knew that such knowledge would in all likelihood have lead to opinions that did not perpetuate Communism.

The danger posed by the widespread ignorance of the Constitution is that it concentrates by default all power and authority in the hands of an elite of unelected federal judges so that the Constitution, in the words of Chief Justice Charles Evans Hughes, becomes nearly "what the judges say it is."

That this line of thinking is beginning to disturb many of us is evident from the Hearst survey finding that 61 percent want a constitutional convention this year to consider amendments on such issues as school prayer, abortion, and freedom of the press.

Clearly, there is a lot everyone needs to learn about the Constitution.

AT ISSUE

*FREEDOM
AND
DEMOCRACY*

RELIGIOUS APARTHEID IN AMERICA

W HEN CONGRESS PASSED the Equal Access Act in 1984, it intended to alleviate discrimination experienced by religious people, most often Christians, who were repeatedly denied opportunities to express their views in public schools. The act permitted religious students to hold after-school Bible studies on school property if the schools also allowed such groups as chess clubs and Future Farmers of America to meet.

But the secularists among us, who argue so forcefully for pluralism in everything else, apparently want God kept completely off public property, even though religious parents pay taxes for school just like everyone else. The after-school-club issue was argued two weeks ago before the Supreme Court, and it will decide later this year the constitutionality of a club formed by a Christian Bible club at Omaha's Westside High School.

It is becoming increasingly clear that there exists in this country a system of religious apartheid that denies religious people full participation in their public institutions as effectively as racial apartheid has denied South African blacks full participation in their country. The difference is that while South Africa has taken the first steps toward racial pluralism, secularists in America are continuing their assault on the public schools.

Religious apartheid began in the early 1960s when prayer and Bible reading in public schools were banned. It has been strengthened through more recent cases that outlawed prayers at public school football games and the use of Christ's name in a valedictorian speech in Louisiana (this case is now being appealed). Also, a Rhode Island judge forbade a rabbi from praying at graduation ceremonies, saying the rabbi's invocation was a prayer because he addressed a deity in the first line and concluded with "Amen." These cases clearly show that the courts repeatedly come down against religious citizens, preferring the secular over the sacred.

This is particularly disturbing since the numerous social problems we confront—drugs, teen-age sex, divorce, abortion—have a spiritual and moral dimension that the secularist "catechism" has failed to successfully address.

If religious citizens want to have an impact on their country, and offer their children more than the limited world view of the secularists, they need to respond to this religious apartheid or risk losing even more freedoms. One strong protest message would be for religious citizens to immediately withdraw their children from public schools and place them in private schools, where high moral values can be reinforced, or educate them at home, a practice that is becoming more popular.

Religious parents who do not take this initiative become tacit accomplices in the plot to secularize the country. We don't send American soldiers to train in the camps of our enemies and expect them to defend our nation and its beliefs and values. Why should religious parents educate their children in a school system that, for example, ignores creation theory in favor of evolution and teaches that sex is an option they can exercise before marriage with no concerns other than preventing venereal disease and pregnancy?

If religious parents want to help their children, they must stop allowing government and public schools to set the standards and think in terms of offering their standards for others to follow. It wasn't religious views and values that gave us a "spiritually vagrant empire" (as theologian Carl Henry has called modern America). It wasn't the imposition of morality found in the Old and New Testaments which brought us so much social blight.

If religious people are looking to the Supreme Court to end religious apartheid, they will be disappointed. Regardless of how the Court rules on after-school clubs, the textbooks have already been purged of the historical values that once were as much a part of America as the religious philosophy that is now banned.

Only a withdrawal from the schools will produce the kinds of "soldiers" who can function in and then return this nation to moral stability. If those who worship an authority higher than the state won't lead the way, rest assured the secularists will.

AT ISSUE

FREEDOM AND DEMOCRACY

TWENTY-ONE

"YOUR MOTHER WEARS ARMY BOOTS"

IF COLORADO DEMOCRATIC Rep. Pat Schroeder and others in her liberal ideological foxhole have their way, women will be assigned to combat roles for the first time in American history. Such a decision would be bad for the military and bad for the country. Most importantly, if women are allowed to be assigned to combat units, the only protection women have enjoyed against the draft would be removed. Should Congress decide to restore the draft because of some future, as yet unforeseen, threat, the courts would surely rule that to exempt women from involuntary service discriminates against men.

Would you want your daughter, sister, wife, or mother to be forced into combat?

The Panamanian operation cited by Schroeder and others as evidence that women can be just as good as men in combat proved nothing. This was a police action, not a rigorous protracted war which our military must always be ready to fight.

A *New York Times* editorial in support of women in combat asks that "both sexes be judged by the same objective standards." Objective standards are appropriate when it comes to assessing mental capabilities or career advancement. But it makes little sense to insist that women in the military demonstrate the same levels of physical strength as men.

Differences in physical strength between men and women have long been recognized by the military. In his book, *Weak Link: The Feminization of the American Military,* Brian Mitchell writes, "All of the services have double standards for men and women on all the events of their regular physical fitness tests. Young male Marines must perform at least three pull-ups to pass the test, but women Marines must only hang from the bar with arms flexed for 16 seconds. In the Army, the youngest women are given an extra three minutes to complete a two-mile run. All the services require men to perform more sit-ups than women, despite the much-vaunted strength of the female midsection."

War is not a golf game where the ladies get a distance advantage on the tee. Why do we acknowledge gender differences in one form of competition—athletics—but not in the ultimate competition—warfare—where the stakes are much higher than a gold medal or a cash prize?

It is because politics has eclipsed reason and sound judgment. The armies of all our potential enemies are almost exclusively male. No other potential enemy has as high a percentage of women in uniform as does the United States. The Soviet Union's 4.4 million-member armed force includes only 10,000 women, and they do mostly clerical and medical work.

The idea of sending women to kill enemy men is contrary to our historical experience, common sense, and American social mores. It would destroy the unique bonding between men in military services that is required for a disciplined, effective fighting force. War is not a social experiment or a proper place for political theories to be tested. Denying women a role in combat does not deny them access to technology or advancement in other military areas.

This nation is not ready for body bags carrying dead females. Continuing to bar women from combat roles is in the best interest of the country. Congress, the Pentagon, and the President ought to put a stop to this bad idea before it advances any more. Otherwise that childhood taunt, "Your mother wears Army boots," might turn out to be true.

AT ISSUE

THE PRESS

THE PRESS

IN 1958, PRESIDENT Dwight Eisenhower was asked by a reporter if the press, during his two terms, had made his job too difficult. The President looked puzzled for a moment, and then responded, "What could *you* possibly do to *me?*" Economist Herb Stein, who recounts the anecdote, adds, "No president since Eisenhower would or could have said that."[1]

Twenty-five years later, David Halberstam, commenting on media coverage of the Vietnam War, boasted, "One correspondent with one cameraman can become as important as 20 senators."[2]

Jack Nelson, Washington bureau chief for the *Los Angeles Times*, asserts, "I don't see any reason why we shouldn't consider ourselves on equal footing with those we cover."[3]

The reason for this dramatic growth in the power of the media, or at least the perception of that growth, is simple. By 1958, the year Eisenhower posed his question, the number of television sets equaled the number of American homes for the first time. The television age had begun. America had a national, visual means of communication, dominated by three networks centered in New York City. Local stations depended on these networks for most of their news and entertainment.

At the same time, the growth of newspaper chains, and the concentration of power in papers like *The New York Times* and *the Washington Post,* reduced the diversity of the daily press. Decisions made in one major newsroom now have national, even international, implications.

Contributing to this centralization of ideas is the decline in the number of newspapers, particularly afternoon papers, in most major and even medium-sized markets. Those that are not shutting down are being gobbled up by giant media conglomerates like *The New York Times* Company and Gannett.

An Elite Corps

One result of these developments was predictable, even inevitable. A few individuals in New York, Washington, and Los Angeles began making decisions that had an immediate impact on millions. Media analysts Thomas Patterson and Ronald Abeles summarize the trend: "Decisions about what the public will know rest increasingly upon the beliefs of a small elite which determines what they should know."[4]

Who are these gatekeepers of information who seem to exercise such influence? According to a recent study by professors Robert Lichter and Stanley Rothman, "On the whole, they are rather homogenous."[5] Ninety-five percent are white. Over 40 percent come from just three states: New York, New Jersey, and Pennsylvania. Most were reared in upper middle-class homes.

David Broder of *The Washington Post* comments, "The fact is that reporters are by no means any kind of cross-section. We are over-educated, we are overpaid in terms of the median, and we have a higher socio-economic stratification than the people for whom we are writing. There is clearly a danger of elitism creeping in."[6] This uniformity extends not only to their background, but to their convictions as well. Exactly half deny any religious affiliation. Only 8 percent go to church or synagogue weekly. Eighty-six percent seldom or never attend religious services.

A majority see themselves as political liberals. Just 17 percent place themselves on the right side of the political spectrum. Over 70 percent have voted for the Democratic candidate in the last six presidential elections. Fully 90 percent believe a woman should have a right to an abortion. Seventy-five percent believe that homosexual practice is morally acceptable. Eighty-five percent say that homosexuals should be allowed to teach in schools. Over 50 percent say there is nothing wrong with adultery.

Lichter and Rothman conclude, "The demographics are clear. The media elite are a homogeneous group, who were raised at some distance from the social and cultural traditions of small-town Middle America. Most have moved away from any religious heritage, and very few are regular churchgoers. Today's leading journalists are politically liberal and alienated from traditional norms and institutions. Most place themselves to the left of center and regularly vote the Democratic ticket. They differ most from the general public on the divisive social issues that have emerged since the 1960s — abortion, homosexual rights, affirmative action. They would like to strip traditional power brokers of their influence and empower black leaders, consumer groups, intellectuals, and . . . the media."[7]

The Development of the Media Elite

When opinion is this uniform, it is tempting to see a conscious and secret conspiracy at work. But the reasons for this general agreement among members of the press and entertainment industries are more complex than that.

This first is simply a matter of environment. Media critic Edward J. Epstein writes, "Producers who tend to read the same newspapers and news magazines, commute to the same area of New York City, and discuss with friends the same agenda of problems can be expected to share a similar perspective on the critical themes of the day."[8]

The second reason is a shared history. A whole new era of young reporters broke into the business during the civil rights movement in the turbulent 1960s. This group began to see journalism as a tool to push for political change that would remedy social injustice. Instead of being observers and chroniclers of events, many of these idealistic young journalists saw themselves as facilitators who could help forge social and foreign policy.

In one study, close to two-thirds of the network correspondents interviewed credited network news for the passage of civil rights legislation. According to one NBC correspondent, "We showed the American public what was happening: the brutality, the police dogs, the miserable conditions blacks were forced to live in. We made it impossible not to act."[9] The trend continued during the critical press treatment of the Vietnam War. Journalists were in constant tension with the Johnson Administration and conveyed their distrust of military and political authority in their stories. While some of this distrust was justified because certain government officials and military spokesmen clearly lied about the prosecution of the war, much of the press overreacted and believed that nothing it was told about the war was true. At one point, following the 1968 Tet offensive, a battle which most would later come to view as a victory for American and South Vietnamese forces, Walter Cronkite used his platform on the "CBS Evening News" to make a personal plea for peace negotiations.

Finally, with the Watergate crisis, this new generation of journalists were confirmed in the conviction of their own power when they took credit for bringing down the Nixon Administration. The image of Bob Woodward and Carl Bernstein and their lonely struggle against corruption, immortalized in the book and film *All the President's Men,* was a compelling model not only to that generation of journalists, but to the next generation who began entering journalism schools in vastly increased numbers.

All this combined to create a certain kind of journalist, as well as a certain kind of journalism. The press developed a distrust of authority, a crusading zeal for liberal progress, a sense of its own power, and, undergirding it all, a conviction that American institutions and standards are oppressive and in need of political reform. Meg Greenfield, editorial page editor of *The Washington Post,* comments:

> Out there—wherever that is—people may be smiling and humming
> . . . but the world according to journalism is, on the contrary, a surpassingly bleak place. A Martian reading about it might in fact suppose America to be composed entirely of abused minorities living in squalid and sadistically run state mental hospitals, except for a small elite of venal businessmen and county commissioners who are profiting from the unfortunates' misery.[10]

The Result of Media Elitism

The profile of the media elite extends beyond journalism. Many of the same arguments could be made concerning the entertainment industry. They are centered in the same areas and are drawn from the same economic class. Writer David Prindle, in a survey of the Screen Actor's Guild, reveals that over 70 percent of the members of this union consider themselves liberal. And, over the last few decades, they have similarly expanded their goals and influence.

Professor Michael Robinson of Catholic University comments, "In the 1950s television was a *reflection* of our social and political opinions, but by the 1960s, it was an important *cause* of them."[11] Television story lines increasingly deal with fashionable progressive issues like AIDS, homosexuality, racism, and abortion, and use the medium to get across the message of social change, according to the liberal worldview. Other programs display a contempt for traditional, and presumably oppressive, social taboos. CBS broadcast a four-hour drama involving incest. Harry Waters of *Newsweek* summarized, "Mother and son embark on a steamy odyssey to Las Vegas, replete with cheek-to-cheek dance embraces and bed-top nuzzlings."[12] Even when it deals with more elevated subject matter, the product is transformed according to a distinct agenda. In prime-time television's version of *Anna Karenina,* she was not consumed (per Tolstoy) with "disgust and horror" over her adultery, but fulfilled by it. Everything was included in the story except the moral.

"The climate of unbelief," according to Harold O. J. Brown, "has created the corruption of culture. "Dallas" and "Dynasty" make sense only in a world in which there is no thought of God or of judgment."[13] And, not surprisingly, these are the admitted characteristics of the media elite.

All of this is somewhat paradoxical. The media elite is a group of economically and culturally privileged people who have moved into strong, even virulent opposition to key American institutions and the values that produced them. They are a minority of the working population, but, as sociologist Peter Burger comments, "They have power in the institutions providing the symbols by which the society understands itself."[14] This alienated and influential group of power-brokers shapes our self-understanding. Senator Daniel Moynihan (D-N.Y.) predicts, "The political consequence of the rising social status of journalism is that the press grows more and more influenced by attitudes genuinely hostile to American society and American government. This trend seems bound to continue in the future."[15]

The Tool of "Public Opinion" Polls

Having been alienated from the culture, much of the press has turned to public opinion polls in an effort to discover the heartbeat of America.

Bill Kovach, curator of the Nieman Foundation at Harvard and a former editor of the *Atlanta Journal-Constitution,* believes that opinion has obscured the pursuit of facts, which used to be journalism's primary concern.

In an op-ed piece for *The New York Times,* Kovach said,

> Every day, one news outlet or another, drawing upon an exclusive poll of public opinion, tells us in great detail what we think about a public issue. And almost every day what they tell us is that we think pretty much what they already have told us about the issues. . . .

> Journalists trained to seek out fact, increasingly have failed to make a distinction between objective, quantifiable fact and opinion. The result has been that ephemeral opinion has, all too often, begun to substitute for objective fact in the diet of information the media provide.[16]

With remarkable honesty, Kovach wrote about the danger of heavy reliance on polling:

> Change the wording of a question and you change the opinion. Change the order of questions and you change opinion. Change the time of day you conduct the poll, and you change the opinion. . . .

> Journalists are moving deeper and deeper into this current, which is subject to violent changes of direction, and we are in danger of losing our footing on the solid ground of objective, demonstrable fact. And we are taking readers and viewers along with us.

> We crowd fact out of the limited space and time of the overall news report and put in its place something less useful, perhaps even misleading. For public opinion is not a public position: It is ill-informed, not thought out. It shifts with each change in information available.[17]

Kovach's indictment is all the more significant because of his role for many years as a press insider. Unfortunately, even as eloquent a critique as his is likely to fall on deaf ears and blind eyes.

AT ISSUE

THE PRESS

PRESS ETHICS COULD USE SOME ATTENTION

Nothing delights the journalistic profession so much as a scandal in someone else's back yard. But when questions of ethics come to call at *our* door, we pretend no one is at home.

Two stories related to ethical standards in journalism came to light recently. Perhaps it was just coincidental that the American Society of Newspaper Editors was holding its convention in Washington when the stories appeared.

The first story involved the often large speaking fees paid to top reporters, columnists, and commentators by organizations. Such fees might have been an object of press criticism had the speaker been a member of Congress. Some journalists (and I am not one of them) receive as much as $25,000 for a single speech, while members of Congress are limited to $2,000 per speech.

The *Washington Post* listed the fees of some of these top talkers along with the excuses of others who refused to disclose their speaking income or its source.

ABC's Sam Donaldson, who is paid plenty for talking on television, refuses to acknowledge the amount or source of his outside income. "I don't hold any public office, nor do I seek one," said Donaldson. "I essentially believe that what I do falls in the nature of private business, just like dentists, doctors, lawyers, and people who run cattle."

Not exactly. How many cattlemen speak to millions of people every night and determine how the news is covered? Some reporters have helped expose wrongdoing by public officials that has led to their removal from office. How many public officials have successfully scuttled the career of a network anchor or newspaper reporter?

We are fond of invading a person's privacy or grief, or reporting the smallest detail concerning alleged wrongdoing. Our defense is "the people's right to know." Don't the people also have a right to know what powerful members of the press make on the side and from whom? If members of the House Banking Committee can be questioned about lecture fees from the savings and loan industry, why isn't it relevant if journalists accept a speaking fee from a group on which they or their network or newspaper might report?

If full disclosure is desirable for politicians, journalists, who also have a responsibility to the public, should lead the way by setting a similar example, and let readers decide whether speaking fees affect their reporting.

Which brings me to the second story related to media ethics.

According to *The Washington Post,* not a few reporters and editors participated in the April 9 abortion rights march on Washington, including Linda Greenhouse of *The New York Times.* Greenhouse covers the Supreme Court, whose members the marchers sought to influence with their demonstration.

The newspaper's written policy specifically prohibits such activity: "The integrity of the *Times* requires that its staff members avoid employment or any other undertakings, obligations, relationships or investments that create or appear to create a conflict of interest with their professional work for the *Times* or otherwise compromises the *Times'* independence and reputation."

The *Post* story indicated that Greenhouse will not be punished, but the incident was used by management to remind the newspaper's employees not to do it again.

Washington Post Executive Editor Ben Bradlee wrote a memo to his staff after hearing that "a number" of *Post* reporters and editors had participated in the march. Bradlee said, "We once again remind members of the newsroom's professional staff that it is unprofessional for you (as opposed to your relatives) to take part in political or issue demonstrations, no matter on which side or how seemingly worthy the cause. It is the choice we make when we choose to work in this business and for this newspaper."

Post employees were told to "recuse yourself from any future participation in coverage of the abortion issue."

It would add considerably to the public's trust of journalists if we would establish some industry-wide guidelines on such matters as speaking fees and participation in news-making events. One veteran editor told me that, in her day, similar violations would not have been tolerated and would have resulted in dismissal. For those who flagrantly abuse journalistic ethics, this is not too high a price.

AT ISSUE

THE PRESS

TWENTY-THREE

NBC'S "ROE V. WADE": SUBTLE PROPAGANDA

FROM THE OPENING SCENE of NBC's movie *Roe v. Wade* to Tom Brokaw's deliberate labeling of two of his guests on an NBC News program as "anti-abortion," instead of "pro-life" as they asked to be called (the other guests were labeled "pro-choice" in accordance with their wishes), America's No. 1 network engaged in a subtle, systematic, and coordinated propaganda campaign.

Anyone who believes that the airing of this film at a time when the Supreme Court is considering a case which could limit or overturn abortion on demand is pure coincidence is a potential customer for a bridge in Brooklyn.

In the film the viewer was carefully led through all of the pro-abortion arguments. Ellen Russell, the character who represented Norma McCorvey (a.k.a. Jane Roe), said, "I got no place to go. I can't give up another baby. What could it possibly be like to have a kid out there gettin' his butt kicked and you don't even know?"

That there were places for unwed mothers to go for care in 1972 was never mentioned.

Was it coincidental that the first commercial, for Maxwell House coffee, featured Linda Ellerbee, who marched in last month's abortion rights demonstration in Washington and who does pro-abortion commentaries on Cable News Network, where she is employed?

The film shifted the focus of attention from the baby to the woman, a strategy that is at the heart of the pro-abortion position. Such a shift is necessary because pro-abortionists have lost the debate over the "humanness" of the baby thanks to ultrasound and fetoscopy, which show clearly fetal development.

The film treated adoption as a less appealing option than abortion, twisting logic and promoting the pro-abortion position that it is more blessed to kill the unborn than it is to enhance three lives, the baby's and couples who desperately want children.

The actress playing attorney Sarah Weddington said to her client, "You shouldn't have to bear a child and give it up to strangers." This is harsh news to the long waiting list of those "strangers," prospective adoptive parents who are hoping that women will indeed give their babies life in order that the lives of barren couples might be enhanced.

There were not-too-subtle references in the film to abortion as a cure-all for welfare (a suggestion that Jesse Jackson once denounced as racist before he converted to the pro-abortion point of view), and there were passing scenes of a dirty abortion table, "intolerant" religion (the Methodist denomination, which favors abortion, received an honorable mention), and insensitive men (except the ones helping the pro-abortion side).

But it was in the hour-long NBC News special following the film that the NBC point of view was stripped of whatever objective clothing remained (on the Washington, D.C., NBC affiliate, a local reporter covering pro-lifers as they watched the movie referred to them as "so-called pro-lifers," while the reporter covering the other side called them "pro-choice").

With body language, smirks, and interruptions, Tom Brokaw quickly revealed his side. Brokaw frequently interrupted and lectured Rep. Chris Smith (R-N.J.) and Olivia Gans of National Right to Life, while allowing Planned Parenthood President Faye Wattleton and author Anna Quindlen to make lengthy uninterrupted responses to questions.

This film and follow-up news program practiced censorship by ignoring the following: a woman deciding not to have an abortion for the baby's sake; people praying about their circumstances (millions do) and receiving counseling and financial help; a crisis pregnancy center (there are hundreds) helping a woman with an unplanned pregnancy before and after the birth of her child, offering her a place to live, food, clothing, medical care, and even a job; pictures of what is being aborted, before and after the fact; interviews with "tough cases" who were not aborted and who are asked whether they wish they had been; interviews with doctors, such as Bernard Nathanson, who used to perform abortions but have "converted" to the pro-life side; interviews with parents whose joy is boundless since they adopted a child.

The pro-abortionists have mounted an unprecedented campaign on radio and television and in newspapers and magazines, hoping to persuade the Supreme Court to leave *Roe v. Wade* alone. They are spending millions. Pro-lifers are spending their smaller resources on saving babies. Who will succeed? No one can be sure. But the verdict is already in from NBC, which has placed itself firmly on the side of death.

AT ISSUE

THE PRESS

THE PRESS AND
THE PANAMA INVASION

SOME JOURNALISTS are complaining that U.S. commanders in Panama kept them from sights "that would detract from what they (the commanders) regarded as a military triumph."

So says Kevin Merida of the *Dallas Morning News,* in a *Washington Post* essay. Merida was one of the pool reporters who accompanied soldiers on the invasion.

". . . military officials either didn't understand or ignored our needs as journalists," complains Merida. "Military commanders were especially eager to promote Noriega as a bizarrely prosperous dictator with a degenerate character." Perhaps that's because Noriega's profile exactly fit that description.

Merida's essay, along with one by George Garneau in *Editor and Publisher* in which he quotes UPI's Matthew Mendelsohn as saying the pool "was a complete and dismal failure," betrays a level of hostility by much of the press that the Pentagon did well to contain.

Panama was the second major battle since Vietnam involving large numbers of American forces in which there have been press restrictions. Grenada was the first. Both operations were military successes that achieved their stated objectives.

The British, during their invasion of the Falkland Islands, also applied restrictions on reporters. That, too, was a successful operation. In the modern era of satellite communication, is there a connection between delaying some of the sardonic musings of the press and the achievement of military objectives? I think there is. Government officials, including the military, must be held accountable by the press, but in the poisoned years following Vietnam and Watergate, some natural press skepticism has evolved into a variety of cynicism that is harming the nation.

Veteran journalists who covered World War II and other pre-Vietnam conflicts remember how things once were.

"You used to know who the enemy was," laments Arnaud deBorchgrave, editor-in-chief of *The Washington Times* and a former foreign correspondent. "Now, the enemy is your own government, and the only reason you want to get in on day one is to report on how our guys screwed up."

Bryson Rash, a former NBC News correspondent, notes that while circumstances were far different in World War II ("there was all-out war and no alternative, and we also had censorship that was never violated except on one or two occasions"), there was a different spirit among journalists of that era and a different attitude toward their own country.

Bob Sherrod, a World War II correspondent for *Time-Life* in the Pacific, tells me, "The relations between the press and the powers were very close. We were all fighting the same war. There was no doubt that the press trusted the high command to a point, and reporters were generally trusted." Sherrod says that Gen. Dwight Eisenhower would brief reporters in advance about an invasion. He also says that Secretary of the Navy James Forrestal advised him in advance of the invasion of Saipan in 1944 so that he could return home in time to write a firsthand story.

No official would dream of doing such a thing today. Such privileged information would probably be broadcasted and printed all over the world by reporters anxious to beat the competition, jeopardizing U.S. policy and the lives of American soldiers.

A glance at reporting during World War II shows a crop of reporters who were a far different breed than some of today's overpaid spoiled brats.

The November 17, 1944, *New York Times* reported "a great offensive against the Reich" and of the advancing soldiers as "our" ground troops.

The same paper carried an editorial that said, "Safe here at home, drying our shoes and overcoats and gloves in front of an open fire or over a radiator, suffering between one dry place and another only the momentary discomfort of a cold and rainy day, what can we do or hope or say to those brave men, fighting and dying in our cause, along the Seigfried Line? We can do each his appointed task, no matter how small, to speed the final victory. We can hope that success will be swift, and the losses small. We can say only, God bless you!"

Imagine such an editorial being written about America and American soldiers today. Instead we often focus on the irresponsible remarks of Ramsay Clark or Jesse Jackson questioning every government policy and every step of the soldiers.

Ernie Pyle, the greatest World War II journalist of them all, did his job so well that he was not only praised by fellow journalists abroad and at home, but by those he covered.

In his book, *The Story of Ernie Pyle,* Lee Miller quotes a letter from Pfc. Robert O'Doherty of the 88th Division: ". . . (Pyle) would do us more good than any high-powered senator in Washington."

Gen. Omar Bradley said of Pyle, "I have known no finer man, no better soldier." And Pyle said, "If I could pick any two men in the world for my father except my own Dad, I would pick Gen. Omar Bradley or Gen. Ike Eisenhower. If I had a son, I would like him to go to Bradley or Ike for advice."

The bravery of American fighting men is undiminished. Unfortunately, responsible journalism and the esteem of too many journalists for their country has been on the decline. Military objectives ought to be policy-driven, not press-driven. Until these priorities are again placed in the right order, it is not a bad idea for the Pentagon to hold reporters at bay, at least until a mission's objectives have a chance to succeed. There will be plenty of time for critiques later.

AT ISSUE

CONGRESS
AND
THE PRESIDENCY

TWENTY-FIVE

WHERE DO CONSERVATIVES GO IN THE 1990s?

THE MAJOR CHALLENGE facing conservatives in the 1990s is to overcome once and for all the stereotype forged in 1948 by liberal Arthur Schlesinger, Jr., a stereotype that has stuck for forty years. Said Schlesinger in an article for *The Nation*: ". . . since the disappearance of Federalism, American conservatives have been characteristically concerned with quick, short-term advantages for themselves and not with the interests of the nation or the welfare of society. A recurrent casualty of the American political culture has been the conservative with high ideals of social responsibility trapped in a plutocratic and shortsighted policy."

This is an unfair generalization to be sure, but filled with enough truth to be an effective weapon for liberals who scored many political victories since the forties by asserting that Republicans were the party of "big business."

But this image can change in the 1990s. Conservatives now face an opportunity and a temptation. If they fall for the temptation, they could lose the advantage they have had in all but one national election since 1968 and forfeit control of the national agenda to liberal Democrats. If they seize the opportunity of leading the world into economic, political, and religious freedom, the American Century will not have been the twentieth. The American Century will be the twenty-first, and it will be conservatives, specifically Republican conservatives, whose ideas and candidates will lead it. Democratic National Chairman Ron Brown indulges in wishful thinking when he asserts that the changes in Europe will "help the Democratic Party immensely." The party of the nuclear freeze, unilateral disarmament, and welfare, not workfare, the party whose Senate Majority leader, George Mitchell, urged President Bush to go to the Berlin Wall and gloat, is not going to benefit from the victories that Republican leadership has brought.

But Republicans could be in danger if they become complacent and self-congratulatory. Housing and Urban Development Secretary Jack Kemp understands this. In an interview in his office, Kemp warned conservatives they must replace their negative strategies with positive ones: "You can't beat a thesis with an antithesis. You've got to have a better thesis."

Kemp said Republicans should be seen as the party of growth and opportunity, while portraying Democrats as the party of redistribution of wealth.

Kemp believes President Bush has played his hand with the Soviets to perfection, but that conservatives could blow the American advantage. While remaining committed to a strong defense, Kemp said, "There is an evolutionary process in the Soviet Union. If conservatives look as if they're trying to take Gorbachev's nose and rub it into the dirt, they'll miss a more profound mission for the United States, which is to manage these changes in such a way as to see them go forward so that perestroika will lead to democratic reforms and, ultimately, free elections in Russia." The West's greatest mistake at the end of World War I was the Treaty of Versailles in which the Germans were humiliated and the seeds were sown for the rise of Hitler and a second world war.

"Every great leader," said Kemp, "has recognized that you earn nothing with a scorched earth policy. The ultimate triumph is the triumph of ideas and allowing the vanquished to see the efficacy of those ideas." Kemp said we "want to change communism, but more importantly we want to replace it with something better. If our only goal is to see the collapse of the Communist movement, we could very well miss a bigger opportunity to see democratic reforms take root in the Soviet Union."

Domestically, where Democrats think they'll fare better than Republicans because of a "peace dividend" they see coming from developments in Europe, the Bush administration has tried to seize the initiative with the president's HOPE proposal (Homeownership and Opportunity for People Everywhere), announced November 10. The major components of the plan include a $2.1 billion matching-grant program to encourage resident ownership of low-income housing, a program to combine housing resources with supportive services for the long-term homeless, and a proposal to allow the use of tax-deferred Individual Retirement Accounts as down payments by first-time home buyers.

While Gorbachev speaks of producing "socialism with a human face," Republicans need to be touting capitalism with a human heart. Kemp believes that is the challenge for conservatives which, if met, will take care of quite a few elections for the foreseeable future.

AT ISSUE

CONGRESS
AND
THE PRESIDENCY

REFORMING ETHICS MEANS TRANSFORMING CONGRESS

R EPUBLICAN NATIONAL Committee Chairman Lee Atwater is not one to blame the current ethics war in Congress on the Democrats alone. Atwater tells me, "The problem is one of arrogance and atrophy. If we had been in control of the House for thirty-five years, we might see things in reverse."

While some predictably talk of using the demise of Jim Wright and Tony Coelho, the Democrats' number one and number three leaders in the House, as a campaign issue in the 1990 election, others are focusing on how to transform a Congress that has become imperialistic in attitude and practice.

The temptation is to concentrate solely on the money — in this case, donations from political action committees (PACs) to members of Congress which help keep them in office and increase special interest influence on legislation. But that's too narrow a target.

What is needed is a systemic reform of Congress, particularly the House of Representatives. It would include but not be limited to an overhaul in the relationship between PACs and members.

The first question ought to be: Just who does the House represent — the people or the members' own interests?

The framers of the Constitution intended that government's three branches would serve as checks on any abuses of power. But as Thomas

G. West, associate professor of politics at the University of Dallas, has written, "when reelection is a virtual certainty, as is now the case, that check is removed."

Writing in *Federalist No. 71*, Alexander Hamilton could have been describing the arrogance of certain members of today's House: "The representatives of the people, in a popular assembly, seem sometimes to fancy that they are the people themselves, and betray strong signs of impatience and disgust at the least sign of opposition from any other quarter; as if the exercise of its rights, by either the executive or judiciary, were a breach of their privilege and an outrage to their dignity."

The key to putting the House back in its place does not lie in conciliatory gestures to the new ruling oligarchy led by the just-installed House Speaker, Tom Foley. It lies with President Bush and the voters.

Only President Bush can make congressional reform a major national issue. But in order to do so, he must replace the "offered hand" with the clenched fist.

The House Democrats' disarray offers Bush a rare opportunity to drive a stake in the heart of the congressional vampire that has been sucking away the lifeblood of the executive branch and dominating foreign and domestic policy for two decades.

At issue is the defense of the presidency against the inroads of an imperialistic Congress. In the past when a president or presidential candidate made Congress the issue, he won. Public revulsion over the congressional pay raise proposal is only the latest example. Whenever Congress and its abuse of power and privilege is the issue, the people and the President prevail.

The goal ought not be to "get" Congress, neither should reform be perceived as totally partisan. Rather, congressional reform ought to be pitched as ultimately beneficial to the people and to Congress.

Again, West states it clearly in a chapter for the book, *The Imperial Congress: Crisis in the Separation of Powers,* when he writes, "The practical heart of a Constitution-restoring presidency will require taking on the Congress. The President will have no quarrel with Congress as a lawmaking body, for that is its proper role. He will, however, do all he can to defeat congressional imperialism against the executive. He will seek or create opportunities to check and roll back the bad habit of con-

gressmen trying to run the executive branch or evading the responsibility of lawmaking."

If President Bush continues to play the lamb and tries to lie down
with the congressional lion, he will be eaten alive. But if he makes his
agenda one of transforming Congress back into the image the founders
had in mind, he will have the support of an overwhelming majority of
the American people.

AT ISSUE

THE SUPREME COURT

THE SUPREME COURT

T HE FRAMERS of the Constitution
took great pains to define and limit the power of the President. They
gave detailed attention to the role and limits of the Congress. But when
they came to the Supreme Court, the Constitution they wrote becomes
suddenly confusing and vague.

The Constitution doesn't, for example, say how many justices
should sit on the high court. It is silent on the power of the Court to
strike down laws as unconstitutional. In fact, its few brief paragraphs on
the Supreme Court say nothing much at all. "The judicial power of the
United States," it says, "shall be vested in one Supreme Court." That
power is defined only as extending "to all Cases, in Law and Equity,
arising under this Constitution."

This open-ended mandate provoked a great deal of debate among
the founders. On one side, some argued that the Constitution had created
a court which would be harmless, precisely because it would be powerless. Alexander Hamilton wrote, "Of the three powers mentioned (the
others being the legislative and executive), the *judiciary* is next to nothing. The judiciary, from the nature of its functions, will always be the
least dangerous to the political rights of the Constitution; because it will
be least in capacity to annoy or injure them . . . . (It) has neither *force,*
nor *will,* but merely judgment."[1] But others predicted a very different
role for the Court. Robert Yates, a prominent Albany lawyer, who was a
contemporary of Hamilton, argued:

The judges under this Constitution will control the legislature, for the Supreme Court is authorized in the last resort to determine what is the extent of the powers of the Congress; they are to give the Constitution an explanation, and there is no power above them to set aside their judgment . . . . There is no authority that can remove them, and they cannot be controlled by the laws of the legislature. In short, they are independent of the people, of the legislature, and of every power under heaven. Men placed in this situation will generally soon feel themselves independent of heaven itself.[2]

How prophetic!

For most of American history, the resolution to this argument seemed clear. Hamilton was vindicated. The Court was, in his words, "beyond question, the weakest of the three departments of power."

The Early Court Decisions

In 1803, the Supreme Court delivered *Marbury v. Madison,* creating, in the absence of specific constitutional instruction, its practice of "judicial review"—the process of determining whether legislation is constitutional. Justice John Marshall, who wrote the majority decision, declared that "an act of the legislature, repugnant to the constitution, is void." But after *Marbury,* the Supreme Court did not hold another federal statute unconstitutional for fifty-six years. The power it claimed, though important, was seldom used.

Decisions by the Court on lesser matters were not even uniformly obeyed. When Thomas Jefferson was ordered by the Supreme Court to hand over his presidential papers and appear in a Richmond court, he simply refused. When the Court decided a land case in favor of an Indian tribe, President Andrew Jackson remarked, "(Chief Justice) John Marshall has made his decision. Now let him enforce it!"[3] Jackson ignored the decision, and it was never put into effect. Abraham Lincoln ignored Chief Justice Taney's writ of habeas corpus during the Civil War, saying, "I must violate one provision of the Constitution so that all the rest may be saved."[4]

The Court was often weak because of the way others viewed it. But most of all, it was inactive because of the way it viewed itself. Justice Nathan Clifford, in 1874, summarized this attitude: "Courts cannot nullify an act of the legislature on the vague ground that they think it opposed to a general latent spirit supposed to pervade or underlie the constitution. . . . Such a power is denied to the courts, because to concede it would be to make the courts sovereign over both the constitution and the people, and convert government into a judicial despotism."[5] Justice Felix Frankfurter, about ninety years later, reflected, "As a member of this court I am not justified in writing my private notions of policy into the Constitution, no matter how deeply I may cherish them or how mischievous I may deem their disregard."[6] In the same year, 1964, Justice John Harlan contended, "The Constitution is not a panacea for every blot on the public welfare. Nor should this Court, ordained as a judicial body, be thought of as a general haven for reform movements."[7]

This view, called "judicial restraint," can be defined simply as the application of the Constitution according to the principles intended by those who ratified the document. A judge, holding this position, would see his job as the impartial application of the law, not the creation of new laws. Robert Bork, refused a position on the Supreme Court largely for holding this position, summarized it this way:

> In a constitutional democracy the moral conduct of the law must be given by the morality of the (constitutional) framer . . . , never by the morality of the judge. The sole task of the latter — and it is a task quite large enough for anyone's wisdom, skill and virtue — is to translate the framer's . . . morality into a rule to govern unforseen circumstances. That abstinence from giving his own desires free play, that continuing and self-conscious renunciation of power, that is the morality of the jurist.[8]

Judicial Activism

This was once the dominant view of constitutional law, but in the 1950s that changed dramatically. From 1953 to 1969, the Supreme Court, headed by Chief Justice Earl Warren, abandoned judicial restraint for judicial activism. In Joseph Sobran's words, "The Supreme Court, conceived originally as a *check* on federal expansion, has turned judicial review into an *instrument* of federal expansion."[9]

This new view was rooted in the work of legal scholars, dissatisfied with merely interpreting the law. Historian Arthur Schlesinger outlined this approach:

> This thesis, crudely put, is that any judge chooses his results and reasons backwards. The resources of legal artifice, the ambiguity of precedents, the range of applicable doctrine, are all so extensive that in most cases in which there is a reasonable difference of opinion, a judge can come out on either side without straining the fabric of legal logic. A naive judge does this unconsciously and conceives himself to be an objective interpreter of the law. A wise judge knows that political choice is inevitable; he makes no false pretense of objectivity and consciously exercises the judicial power with an eye to political results.[10]

Justice William O. Douglas, a chief proponent of judicial activism on the Warren Court, was a prime example of this new approach. Douglas once confessed that he would rather create a precedent than find one and said his opinions were guided by his "gut." "At the constitutional level where we work, 90 percent of any decision is emotional," said Douglas. "The rational part of us supplies the reasons for supporting our predilections."[11]

"The judiciary's great achievement of our times," writes Joseph Sobran, "has been to turn the great and permanent charter of American liberty into an instrument of utterly unpredictable inventions."[12] The activist intentions of the Warren Court and its philosophical descendants pervaded every area of American life. They dictated national policy forbidding school prayer, expanding the rights of criminals, preventing aid to private schools, defending the legal distribution of pornography, forcing school busing, ending restrictions on birth control, and, finally, declaring abortion a constitutional right. Patrick Buchanan comments, "Since the mid-1950s, using its power to 'interpret' the Constitution, the Supreme Court has literally remade the face of America. The Left has never had so powerful an ally."[13]

This kind of activism was justified as an attempt to "expand" individual rights, "broaden" constitutional protections and "discover" new implications of established legal doctrines. Some even defended it as an attempt to correct the "infirmities" of representative institutions and the "timidities" of elected officials by addressing "unmet social needs."

"But this principle," argues George Will, "is a close cousin to another one: Courts should take their bearing from social judgments and political outcomes."[14]

Professor Alexander Bickel calls this

> an assault on the legal order by moral imperatives [which] came from within, in the Supreme Court headed for fifteen years by Earl Warren. More than once, and in some of its most important actions, the Warren Court got over doctrinal difficulties or issues of the allocation of competences among various institutions by asking what is viewed as a decisive practical question: If the Court did not take a certain action which was 'right' and 'good,' would other institutions do so, given political realities? The Warren Court took the greatest pride in cutting through legal technicalities, in piercing through process to substance.[15]

Activist judges have defended the judicial revolution of the last few decades as the triumph of "constitutional values" — implied, not stated, in the Constitution itself. "But," argues Sobran, "nobody should be fooled. The Court "discovered" these values in the Constitution at just the same time the organs of liberal propaganda were pushing them, and those Justices who dominated the court at the peak of its liberalism . . . were also, in their personal lives, passionate advocates of liberal causes. They were promoting their own policy preferences when they pretended to be reading the Constitution, and they got away with it."[16]

Roe v. Wade

The height of this kind of activism came with *Roe v. Wade* in 1973. This was after the Warren years, but the constitutional theory continued to haunt the Court like Warren's ghost. Justice Harry Blackmun, writing for the majority, claimed to have discovered a right to privacy in a "penumbra" of the Constitution that applied to abortion and struck down abortion laws in all fifty states.

Robert Bork comments, "The Court did not even feel obliged to settle the question of where the right to privacy or the subsidiary right to abort is to be attached to the Constitution's text. The opinion seems to regard that as a technicality that really does not matter, and indeed it does not, since the right does not come out of the Constitution but is forced into it. . . . This is not legal reasoning, but fiat."[17]

Justice Byron White, dissenting in *Roe,* argued,

> I find nothing in the language or history of the Constitution to support the Court's judgment. The Court simply fashions and announces a new constitutional right for pregnant mothers and, with scarcely any reason or authority for its action, invests that right with sufficient substance to override most existing state abortion statutes. . . . As an exercise of raw judicial power, the Court perhaps has the authority to do what it does today; but in my view its judgment is an improvident and extravagant exercise of the power of judicial review.[18]

Roe v. Wade represents the clearest example of the Court pursuing its own liberal agenda, under the pretense of interpreting the Constitution. "In the years since 1973," Bork comments, "no one, however proabortion, has ever thought of an argument that even remotely begins to justify *Roe v. Wade* as a constitutional decision." The justifications are "not legal but moral."[19] The Court, it seems, had finally come to the point which Robert Yates feared. "In short, they are independent of the people, of the legislature, and of every power under heaven."[20]

The consequences for a democracy are profound. Important decisions are taken out of the hands of voters and put in the hands of unelected judges. "If this is all that judges do," wrote Bickel, "then their authority over us is totally intolerable and totally irreconcilable with the theory and practice of democracy."[21] Justice Hugo Black, who was occasionally guilty of the sin he condemns, warned that the nation could "cease to be governed by the law of the land and instead become one governed ultimately by the rule of judges."[22] He preferred to put his "faith in the words of the written Constitution itself rather than to rely on the shifting, day-to-day standards of fairness of individual judges."[23] Abraham Lincoln said that under an activist Court, "the people will have ceased to be their own rulers, having to that extent practically resigned their Government into the hands of that eminent tribunal."[24]

Supporters of judicial restraint have urged the Court to return these questions to the voters. And with new appointments to the Supreme Court, that process may have begun. The Court's 1989 abortion case, *Webster v. Reproductive Health Services,* returned limited authority to the states to restrict abortion. The decision began a firestorm of debate between pro-lifers and pro-abortionists that will not soon subside.

But this raises one final difficulty. Alexander Bickel once said, "If men are told complacently enough that this is how things are, they will become accustomed to it and accept it. And in the end, this is how things will be."[25]

Since the 1950s, the agenda of activist courts has been forced on the American public. And for over seventeen years, Americans have become accustomed to abortion-on-demand. When decisions on such issues are taken from the courts and handed back to the public, it is not at all certain how they will respond. The reaction to *Webster* has been mixed, and the political situation is unclear.

Americans have dealt with corrupted courts for decades. But changing those courts may not have the effect for which many had hoped. We may well be left with corrupted voters. "The effect of liberty to individuals," wrote Edmund Burke, "is that they may do what they please."[26]

We ought to see what it will please them to do, before we risk congratulations.

AT ISSUE

THE SUPREME COURT

WHAT THE DEBATE OVER THE SUPREME COURT IS ALL ABOUT

WHEN LEWIS POWELL resigned from the Supreme Court, he sparked a great debate over "judicial philosophy." An important part of the debate has been identifying judges and justices by their approach to the law.

Invariably, judges favored by liberals are described by them as "moderates" or "centrists." Those disdained by liberals are labeled "ultra conservatives," "right wingers," "ultra right wingers," "extremists," or "ideologues."

What do these powerful words mean? For one thing they can enhance or detract from a judge's candidacy for the Supreme Court. "Moderates" or "centrists"—or "pragmatic centrist," as *The New York Times* called Justice Powell—seem to describe those who wish to use the courts as a means of social change. One *Times* editorial called for the President to fill Powell's seat with someone from the "modern mainstream," whatever that means.

Adding to the confusion is the fact that while liberals tend to resemble one another in philosophy and agenda, conservatives do not.

The Reagan Administration frequently describes judges it favors for the federal bench as "judicial conservatives."

Tayt Dencer, special counsel for the conservative legal organization, The Rutherford Institute, says judicial conservatives make a distinction between facts and values. Those who follow this philosophy take a detached and clinical approach to the Constitution as they consider only the facts in a case. In this view, values have no place in the law. This is known as the "law and economics" school of thought, taught at the Chicago Law School, a training ground for many of the Reagan Administration's judicial nominees.

So the battle lines are drawn between those who believe the law serves to ratify sociological change and those who believe that the law establishes and protects a universal standard to which all should conform to promote the general welfare.

The true conservative jurist sees himself as a steward of the law, because law has a source, a lawgiver. He does not make the law. The liberal activist judge sees law, like Man, as part of an evolutionary process, in need of direction from a higher authority, which he sees as his role.

Such a view inevitably leads to what has been described as sociological law. And so, as the late Francis Schaeffer and Surgeon General C. Everett Koop observed in their book, *Whatever Happened to the Human Race*:

> Law is only what most of the people think at that moment of history, and there is no higher law. It follows, of course, that the law can be changed at any moment to reflect what the majority currently thinks.

> More accurately, the law becomes what a few people in some branch of government think will promote the present sociological and economic good. In reality the will and moral judgment of the majority are now influenced by, or even overruled by the opinions of, a small group of men and women. This means that vast changes can be made in the whole concept of what should and what should not be done. Values can be altered overnight and at almost unbelievable speed.

Law, then, has become utilitarian. It can be what the majority conceives as law, or it can be what an elite says it is. There is no absolute.

These are the two underlying ideological currents, running in opposite directions and incapable of meeting, that drive the tumultuous debate over the future of the Supreme Court. Questions for Judge Anthony Kennedy should center not just on how he has ruled in cases, but in which of these two categories he ruled.

AT ISSUE

THE SUPREME COURT

JUSTICE MARSHALL AND THE CONSTITUTION

J USTICE THURGOOD MARSHALL is both right and wrong in his recent critique of the Constitution before a group of lawyers meeting in Hawaii.

But more than anything else, his comments showed the arrogance of some Supreme Court justices who seem to think all too little of tampering with a document that has worked for two hundred years.

Marshall is right in his criticism that the founding fathers believed liberty and equality were to be the exclusive preserve of white males, but he is wrong in his assertion that "the government [the framers] devised was defective from the start."

As flawed as the nation's beginning may have been, the framers of the Constitution drew on certain absolutes which led to the freedoms that women, blacks, and others now enjoy. These freedoms might never have emerged had our government been founded on the shifting sands of arbitrary law and subjective judgments that characterize modern jurisprudence.

Marshall said in his speech: "I do not believe that the meaning of the Constitution was forever 'fixed' at the Philadelphia convention."

But the Constitution's real strength, overlooked by Marshall, is derived from its grounding in a set of fixed absolutes. This has made it a self-correcting document. Because of this unique quality, those who were once oppressed enjoy nearly equal opportunities today. It is also why this document has sustained the greatest experiment in freedom and self-government the world has ever known.

The framers did not conceive the Constitution in an ideological vacuum. They drew heavily on the writings of Samuel Rutherford (1600–61), a Scotsman who wrote *Lex Rex,* which means law is king. This was a revolutionary notion, for until that time government had been *rex lex*—the king is law.

Rutherford believed the heads of government should be under the law, not a law unto themselves. This view, later refined by John Locke, heavily influenced Thomas Jefferson to write of "certain inalienable rights endowed by our Creator" and of "self-evident truths."

But by the twentieth century, Chief Justice Frederick Moore Vinson (1946–53) would write that "nothing is more certain in modern society than the principle that there are no absolutes."

Blaming the framers and the Constitution they wrote for the social evils which Justice Marshall rightly bemoans would be like blaming God and the Bible for the Crusades or the PTL Club scandal. In each case, the authors posited some solid principles. It was the interpreters who misapplied them.

Justice Marshall and his liberal colleagues on the Supreme Court have now become a law unto themselves. The result has been sociological law, which evolves to fit the opinion polls or the whims of a handful of judges.

In his critique, Justice Marshall referred to the Constitution's twenty-six amendments as a weakness. He implied that the amendments were an attempt to right certain wrongs in the original articles. While this is true in matters of race and gender, the amendment process is also one of the document's great strengths.

As constitutional attorney William Bentley Ball has said, "We misconstrue the Constitution if we believe it is really an instrument to be constantly rewritten according to subjective judgments which may be the product of social movements." Rather than relying upon the amendment process, says Ball, the Supreme Court has taken upon itself *rex lex* days that preceded John Witherspoon. But rather than a single king, we now have nine "kings" sitting in black robes, telling us what the law is.

The government of "we the people," as envisioned by the framers, no longer exists. It has been replaced with a government of "we the Justices."

AT ISSUE

EDUCATION

SCHOOLS AND TEXTBOOKS GET "F" IN DEMOCRACY

ALLAN BLOOM, author of *The Closing of the American Mind,* was correct to subtitle his best-selling book: *How Higher Education Has Failed Democracy and Impoverished the Souls of Today's Students.*

According to a report released by the American Federation of Teachers (AFT), public schools have failed democracy by not teaching students how to understand and appreciate it.

Called "Democracy's Untold Story: What World History Textbooks Neglect," the report is an indictment of an education establishment that has been more interested in fulfilling the agendas of special interest groups than in teaching students about democratic values and explaining why they work better than other governmental systems.

Lynne Cheney, chairwoman of the National Endowment for the Humanities and an AFT study panel member, says a major problem in writing the textbooks is that the authors consult a checklist of one hundred guidelines that must be observed in any book for public school use. No wonder both conservative and liberal critics have indicted textbooks for being "dumbed down."

For example, not one of the five history textbooks examined in the study explains or gives more than a mention of the writings of Plato and Aristotle. The report said, "The basic idea of Judaism and Christianity, which inform every debate over right and wrong and the place of the individual in society, are all but ignored in some of these texts and only feebly suggested in the rest."

The panel called the history texts used in more American schools bland, incomplete, lacking drama, and more interested in developing study skills than in presenting ideas.

Why is this so?

Ruth Wattenberg, who chaired the study panel for the American Federation of Teachers, says textbook writers overreacted to the universally favorable view of America and democracy contained in books of the 1930s and 40s. Now, she says, the pendulum has swung to the other extreme. It is almost as if we are embarrassed to praise democracy.

And this failure to provide stimulating and wide-ranging texts is producing disastrous results in students. An October 1985 study for the National Endowment for the Humanities found that by the time our children reach their senior year in high school, one-half do not recognize the names Churchill and Stalin; two-thirds cannot place the Civil War in the correct half-century; one-third do not know that the Declaration of Independence was signed between 1750 and 1800; one-half cannot locate the half-century in which World War I occurred; and one-third do not know that Columbus sailed for the New World before 1750.

Prof. Paul Gagnon of the University of Massachusetts, Boston, who wrote the report, says a major reason why our children are not learning more history is the lack of unifying themes. He and Ruth Wattenberg say that teachers must be provided with new lesson plans to allow them to supplement inferior history texts until writers and publishers are able to improve the basic resource material.

Tocqueville observed that the great danger to democracy is its enslavement to public opinion. There has been too much emphasis placed on what the special interest groups want and not nearly enough on what a student needs to become an educated adult. We are producing a generation of students who have been indoctrinated but not educated; who can repeat information, but who are unable to think critically because they lack a historically based worldview.

AFT President Albert Shanker says, "We are not talking about cheerleading. We are talking about thinking, about understanding our ideals, about knowing our past—the unfortunate and the evil as well as the good. That is not indoctrination. That is education in the best sense of the word."

And that is precisely what is missing in our history books and in our culture. It is why intellectual development of children in America has virtually ceased in favor of hours spent in front of the television set.

AT ISSUE

EDUCATION

SCHOOL-BASED CLINICS: A PRESCRIPTION FOR DISASTER

THE NEWEST FRANCHISE with enormous growth potential has nothing to do with hamburgers or carpet cleaning. It is the school-based clinic, 119 of which are now in operation, dispensing birth control devices to American high school students. One can envision a McDonald's-like sign outside the high schools one day: "Billions and billions served."

School-based clinics are touted by their supporters as the best way to deal with the more than one million teen-agers who become pregnant each year. The United States, which is losing economic ground to other nations, has the dubious distinction of being first in teen pregnancies among Western countries.

Those who are pushing for school-based clinics contend that they will reduce unwanted pregnancies among teen-agers. But proponents of the clinics do not have the facts on their side.

New research underwritten by a Ford Foundation grant at Grady Memorial Hospital in Atlanta shows a special health education program for eighth-grade girls led to a substantial decline in sexual involvement.

The program focuses on girls from low-income families, the category which produces the highest rate of teen-age pregnancies.

The centerpiece of the Grady Hospital program is not condoms or pills. Rather, the program provides physiological information, helps the girls confront peer pressure, and heavily emphasizes "just saying no" to sex. Those who have given up on such an approach as "impractical" ought to know that 97 percent of the students in the Atlanta program felt the information they received would help them personally in saying "no" to sex.

Since the emphasis was on postponing sexual involvement, not preventing pregnancy, the Grady program diverges from the goal of school-based clinics. Their goal presumes sexual involvement and seeks only to prevent its physical consequences. (They are unsuccessful in this, too, as we'll see in a moment.)

Fifteen percent of the eighth-grade girls in the study who did not participate in the Atlanta program became sexually involved by the end of the school year. But only 5 percent of those in the program became sexually active. The net result was that two out of every three girls who ordinarily might have become sexually involved postponed it.

Reporting last year on a national study he conducted, Stan E. Weed, director of the independent Institute for Research and Evaluation in Salt Lake City, said,

> As the number and proportion of teen-age family-planning clients increased, we observed a corresponding increase in the teen-age pregnancy and abortion rates: 50 to 120 more pregnancies per thousand clients, rather than the 200 to 300 fewer pregnancies as estimated by researchers at the Alan Guttmacher Institute (formerly the research arm of Planned Parenthood). We did find that greater teen-age participation in such clinics led to lower teen *birthrates* [emphasis his]. However, the impact on the abortion and total pregnancy rates was exactly opposite the stated intentions of the program. The original problems appear to have grown worse.

So it is obvious what is needed instead of school-based clinics is a determined attempt to educate young people to the value of just saying "no" to sex and to rebuild the demolished moral ethic that leads to teen-age sex in the first place.

For those who desire a powerful weapon in opposing the proliferation of school-based clinics, a new book by Barrett L. Mosbacker,

School Based Clinics and Other Critical Issues in Public Education (Crossway Books), provides plenty of facts.

Failure to instill in our children a code of moral ethics has led to the ethical chaos we now deplore in politics, economics, and even religion.

ABC's Ted Koppel charted the way back to this ethical imperative in his commencement speech at Duke University in 1987: "We have actually convinced ourselves that slogans will save us. Shoot up if you must, but use a clean needle. Enjoy sex whenever and with whomever you wish, but wear a condom. No! The answer is no! Not because it isn't cool or smart, or because you might end up in jail or dying in an AIDS ward. But no because it's wrong. . . ."

As the Grady Hospital experiment and the Stan Weed study have shown, that kind of ethic, and not school-based clinics, will work.

AT ISSUE

EDUCATION

WHAT HAPPENED TO "THE FREEDOM TO READ"?

W AS IT ONLY A SHORT time ago that "fundamentalist" Christian parents in Tennessee were under attack by "tolerant, pro-academic freedom, pluralistic" liberals for objecting to the teaching of certain ideas in public school textbooks and reading materials? These parents were said to oppose stories such as *The Wizard of Oz* on grounds that it flirted with witchcraft and *The Diary of Anne Frank* because it exposed their children to pantheism. To the guardians of academic thought, censorship was at issue and the freedom to read what the state and its representatives believed important was paramount.

Now comes one of those "the shoe is on the other foot" cases in which the freedom-to-read concept has been thrown to the winds in favor of a naked attempt at book banning.

The case involves a book approved for sale by the California Bicentennial Commission of the United States Constitution. State legislators have demanded (yes, demanded) that Gov. George Deukmejian dismiss the appointees to the commission for approving a history textbook that includes a 1934 essay on slavery referring to black children as "pickaninnies" and saying that the "constant fear of slave rebellion" made life for Southern whites "a nightmare."

Though Deukmejian has launched an investigation into the matter, sale of the book, *The Making of America*, which was used to raise money for California's observance of the Constitution's two hundredth anniversary, was halted. The authors have labeled criticism of the book "ludicrous," but there is a larger point which is being overlooked.

Several years ago there was a controversy over whether children should be allowed to read *The Adventures of Huckleberry Finn* because of author Mark Twain's frequent use of the word "nigger." Never mind that Twain's intent was to attack racial hatred and stereotyping. The word itself had been declared out of bounds by some members of the thought police.

I have not read *The Making of America,* but would it not be possible to use half-century-old references to race as a discussion tool on the evils of racism rather than employ them as a disqualifier?

And what about the pure-as-snow doctrine of the freedom-to-read folks, which appears so virginal as to tolerate no deviation?

Liberals are fond of referring to a joint statement released nearly forty years ago by the American Library Association (ALA) and the Association of American Publishers. That statement, entitled "The Freedom to Read," set forth the associations' view of attempts to censor books: "The freedom to read is essential to our democracy. It is continuously under attack. Private groups and public authorities in various parts of the country are working to remove books from sale, to censor textbooks, to label 'controversial' books, to distribute lists of 'objectionable' books or authors, and to purge libraries. These actions apparently arise from a view that our national tradition of free expression is no longer valid. . . ." In its 1948 "Library Bill of Rights," the ALA said, "Materials should not be excluded because of the origin, background, or views of those contributing to their creation." And, in a 1971 "Interpretation" of the document, the ALA said, "We will make available to everyone who needs or desires them the widest possible diversity of views and modes of expression, *including those which are strange, unorthodox, or unpopular* (emphasis mine)."

People for the American Way (PAW), a self-appointed anti-censorship organization that includes many prominent Americans, has attacked conservatives when they object to the content of some books. PAW's President Anthony Podesta has said of such objections from the right, "In other words it's dangerous for people to be left to the task of thinking and sorting things out for themselves; they might come to conclusions different from those sanctioned by the government."

PAW is one of the groups leading the effort to keep Californians from sorting things out for themselves and which wants to ban *The Making of America,* apparently out of fear that readers might come to different conclusions than those sanctioned by the government.

It was precisely for such two-faced positions that the word hypocrisy was invented.

INDIVIDUAL RIGHTS OR RESPONSIBILITIES?

THIRTY-TWO

WHY LIBERALS WON'T PROTECT THE FLAG

REMEMBER THE 1984 Democratic National Convention in San Francisco? The hall looked like the flag factory George Bush visited during the 1988 campaign. San Francisco Democrats sought to visually trump the Republicans, whom they had accused of "wrapping themselves in the flag." By golly, Democrats would show they could out-flag-wrap the Republicans.

The hypocrisy of that ploy is now revealed by the stands of many Democrats against a constitutional amendment to protect the flag. These Democrats say such an amendment is "over-reacting," as if to suggest that flag burning is rational behavior. Democrats are saying that conservatives should be ashamed for wanting to protect the flag. Yet despite all their flag waving, Democrats have not been able to escape their association in many people's minds with the radical Left, who demonstrated their revulsion for America by burning her flag and appeared comfortable waving (or keeping company with those who waved) the Viet Cong, North Vietnamese, PLO, Nicaraguan, Cuban, Soviet, or Chinese flags instead.

The Left's favorite historian, Arthur Schlesinger, Jr., weighed in on the flag-burning debate with an essay in *The New York Times Book Review* in which he accurately, if accidentally, gets to the heart of the issue about whether the flag should be protected from those who would do it harm.

Schlesinger writes:

> The very word *desecration* implies that the American flag is sanctified, an object of worship. . . .

> We are witnessing the rise of what Charles Fried, Ronald Reagan's solicitor general, calls the "doctrine of civil blasphemy." Whether religious or secular in guise, all forms of blasphemy have in common that there are things so sacred that they must be protected by the arm of the state from irreverence and challenge—that absolutes of truth and virtue exist and that those who scoff are to be punished.

It is Schlesinger's and his fellow scoffers' belief that there is no absolute truth (civil rights?) or virtue (honesty?) that has brought us to the abyss. Our nation is suffering from the moral equivalent of waste washing up on the shore because of our reluctance to uphold what once were self-evident truths, a phrase the historian Schlesinger ought to appreciate.

The danger that comes from the Supreme Court's flag-burning decision is not to the flag (which could be protected by mandating that all flags be made of flame-resistant material), but rather, in the words of the Pledge of Allegiance, ". . . to the Republic for which it stands."

Freedom requires an anchor; otherwise, it quickly becomes license. Freedom presumes responsibility to a standard, a code. License requires nothing but a desire to slake one's own thirst, no matter the consequences to one or to many. Freedom has a price, and the flag is a symbol of that price, paid for by a currency of blood from thousands of soldiers. License wants the benefits of freedom without the cost.

Sen. Bob Kerry (D-Neb.) warned his fellow Senators that most Americans don't "understand what is potentially at stake if our Bill of Rights is altered." But it is the Supreme Court itself that has been altering not only the Bill of Rights, by protecting pornographers and establishing secularism as the official religion, but also by altering the rest of the Constitution as well (abortion, affirmative action, etc.). True friends of the Constitution want to repair the damage, not cause more.

Erosion, whether in nature or in a culture, is a slow process. Tolerance of marijuana paved the way for crack cocaine. Topless pinups led to the kinds of pornography that inspire serial killers. Elvis opened the musical door through which heavy metal and garbage-mouthed groups eventually walked.

The proposed constitutional amendment to prohibit the flag's desecration is an opportunity to say that enough has finally become enough, that the relativism in which Arthur Schlesinger, Jr., believes has hurt, not helped, America.

AT ISSUE

INDIVIDUAL RIGHTS
OR
RESPONSIBILITIES?

THIRTY-THREE

WHAT'S WRONG
WITH A WAITING PERIOD
FOR GUNS?

RESPONSIBLE GUN OWNERS have always resisted any laws that would ban guns completely, saying that if guns are outlawed, only outlaws will have guns. But the shooting of thirty-four children and a teacher in Stockton, California (five of the children died), and the wounding of four students at Woodrow Wilson High School in Washington nine days later, demands that another look be taken at this argument about laws and guns and human nature.

If banning guns is not possible, then how about at least requiring a waiting period of up to two weeks for those who apply to purchase a gun?

Our nation is drowning in sex and violence. Often the two are related, as serial killer Ted Bundy testified before his execution. The next television season will feature programs of simulated violence which some critics have dubbed "slash TV." Sick minds are influenced by this material to perform violent acts.

Some merchants are all too eager to cash in on our national preoccupation with violence.

In Fairfax County, Virginia, just outside Washington, an F. W. Woolworth store has fifteen Chinese-made, AKS-762 rifles for sale. The advertised price for this "gun of the month" was four hundred dollars. The weapon, a version of the AK-47 paramilitary rifle, is similar to the one used in the California shootings. It can fire six hundred rounds per minute and is designed for the sole purpose of killing people.

Why is Woolworth's, a family store, selling such weapons?

It is small consolation to the dead and wounded in Stockton and Washington that the rights of people to keep and bear arms are being protected.

The Federal Bureau of Alcohol, Tobacco and Firearms estimates there are 50,000 military semiautomatics in the United States. The agency says 88,000 AK-47s and 102,000 Uzis have been imported since 1985. There are no figures available on other brands of automatic and semiautomatic weapons.

Conservatives are beginning to join liberals in a much-needed coalition to gang up on the open-ended proliferation of guns in our nation.

California governor George Deukmejian, a conservative Republican who was elected in 1982 as a foe of gun control, now says he supports a law requiring a fifteen-day waiting period to buy any firearm.

Los Angeles police chief Daryl Gates wants to get assault rifles completely off the streets.

Senator Howard Metzenbaum (D-Ohio) wants to ban further manufacture and importation of such weapons while subjecting existing ones to registration and tight regulations on transfer.

The waiting period seems most likely to win a consensus from all political corners. It would serve two purposes. If the buyer is angry or disturbed, a waiting period would allow cool-off time. It would also permit the applicant for the gun to be thoroughly checked against police records. Patrick Purdy, who shot the schoolchildren in Stockton, lied about his police record and mental stability on a gun application form, but there was no waiting period, and no one verified his answers.

Laws may not deter everybody, but they do deter some people. If just a single incident like the one in Stockton or in Washington can be prevented, it won't hurt responsible gun lovers to suffer a little inconvenience. After all, the dead and wounded students and their families have suffered the ultimate inconvenience.

AT ISSUE

INDIVIDUAL RIGHTS
OR
RESPONSIBILITIES?

MORE PRISONS
NOT THE ANSWER
TO CRIME CONTROL

P RESIDENT BUSH'S announcement
that he would ask Congress for $1.2 billion for fighting crime, $1 billion
of which is designated for the construction of new prisons, might bring
him some support from conservatives, but it will not reduce criminal
activity.

Early in life most people stop believing in Santa Claus and the tooth
fairy, but some grow old and die clinging to the fiction that the way to
stop crime is to build more prisons, impose longer sentences, and "get
criminals off the streets." This view assumes that criminals, like endangered species, are a fixed number, and by imprisoning those currently
committing crimes there will be none left to commit more.

If more prisons resulted in less crime, the United States might rank
as the most crime-free nation on earth, because we have a staggeringly
high incarceration rate — right behind the Soviet Union and South Africa.
Today, 244 of every 100,000 Americans are in prison. This is ten times
the imprisonment rate of the Netherlands, seven times that of Japan and
four times that of West Germany. Moreover, the U.S. prison population
has doubled since the last decade (to more than 627,000) and is increasing fifteen times faster than the general population.

However, as the prison population grows, so does the crime rate. In 1987 the prison population grew by 7.2 percent. In 1988 there was a 7.4 percent jump. In 1987, the last year for which figures are available, incidents of crime went up 2 percent, according to the FBI. If those who believe more prisoners mean fewer crimes being committed were right, crime should have declined in something roughly equivalent to the increase in the prison population.

Politicians, Republicans and Democrats alike, seem to ignore the figures and simply use the issue of crime as an opportunity to talk tough.

While campaigning for president in 1980, Jimmy Carter said that a "great contribution to the crime rate in this country (is) because of Watergate, because of the CIA revelations, and because of the disgraceful actions of the FBI."

I never heard a bank robber say that Richard Nixon made him do it.

In 1976 Ronald Reagan told the California Police Officers Association, "We must put on the back burner the idea of reforming and rehabilitating criminals and get back on the front burner the idea of prosecuting, punishing, and putting them away." President Gerald Ford told the International Association of Chiefs of Police in 1974, "We must take the criminal out of circulation. . . . We must ensure that swift and prolonged imprisonment will inevitably follow each and every offense. Only then will we deter others from pursuing careers of crime."

Studies show prisons are not cost-effective, and the taxpayers are not getting their money's worth. For every dollar currently spent on prison construction, American taxpayers will spend an additional $12.50 in operating costs over the next thirty years.

Expenditures for yearly operating costs are generally cited as being between $10,000 and $20,000 *per cell.* New prisons cost as much as $80,000 per cell to construct and staff. These costs do not include the wider financial impact on society of incarcerating people, which at the very least consists of lost employment taxes and welfare payments to the families of prisoners. And still crime increases. So, what's the answer?

The answer lies in a revival of the 1983 Sentencing Improvement Act, co-authored by Sens. Sam Nunn (D-Ga.) and William Armstrong (R-Colo.). For nonviolent and nondangerous offenders, the bill proposes that society's interests are better served through the imposition of alternative sentences, such as restitution and community service.

The measure would establish a presumption that imprisonment is not appropriate for offenses which do not involve the threat or use of force, endanger national security, or threaten or cause serious physical harm to others.

Restitution would require an offender to repay the victim of his crime for property lost or personal damages sustained as a result of the offender's acts. One-half the federal prison population consists of nonviolent, nondangerous offenders. They ought to be put to work, paying back their victims, not languishing in prison cells, subsidized by the taxpayers. Currently, a victim gets little or nothing, and the taxpayers pay for a system that often serves as more of a training school for criminals than a rehabilitation center.

Why should small-time embezzlers, bad-check writers, and petty burglars be in prison when they ought to be working to pay back those they have wronged, benefitting both the victim and society? That's the road to real justice.

PART THREE

ISSUES EXTERNAL

★ ★ ★

AMERICA
AND WORLD AFFAIRS

AT ISSUE

EASTERN EUROPE

THE SOVIET UNION

ADVOCATES OF THE Cold War theory have been holding "going-out-of-business sales" ever since Mikhail S. Gorbachev became the first among equals in the Communist Party of the Soviet Union.

If one were to select a date which marked the beginning of the end of the forty-year Cold War period between the United States and the Soviet Union, it must be December 8, 1988, in New York City.

It was the day Gorbachev took Manhattan.

Gorbachev's announced purpose for the visit was a speech at the United Nations. He dazzled the delegates (and his intended American audience) by promising cuts in Soviet troops and tanks in Europe. But it was Gorbachev's style, not his modest substance, which captivated Americans and which has seduced much of the world.

The images were unprecedented for a Soviet leader. An early joke about the young and attractive Raisa Gorbachev said that she was the first wife of a Soviet leader to weigh less than her husband. And Gorbachev, himself, is known more for his smile than the furrowed and bushy brows of most of his predecessors.

Gorbachev looks and behaves more like a man of the West than a man from the East. He pumped hands on Fifth Avenue like a New York mayor seeking votes in a campaign. He bantered with reporters, many of whom had never seen a Soviet leader up close and personal. He waved and smiled to admiring crowds. America had met her enemy and, behold, he looked just like us. Perhaps, some thought, he is not an enemy at all. If we didn't know better, he might have been a balding, genial candidate for city council. Decades of distrust seemed to melt away with every photo opportunity — culminating with President Reagan, future President Bush, and Gorbachev chatting amiably. The Statue of Liberty served as a background prop.

In the shadow of "the Lady," as Reagan often referred to the statue, one of America's most consistent and oldest enemies of communism shook rhetorical holy water on Gorbachev and offered him the absolution of a priest. Reagan called Gorbachev "a new kind of Soviet leader."

Almost overnight, public opinion shifted. Before Gorbachev's visit, 60 percent of Americans still thought of the Soviet Union as a serious threat to our national security. After the visit 54 percent said that the Soviet threat was either minor or nonexistent. Crowds all over the world now chant "Gorby, Gorby, Gorby," as if Gorbachev is an Olympic athlete who deserves the strength of the crowd before entering his event. Imagine anyone doing that for Stalin or Brezhnev.

In West Germany, with Soviet troops just across the border, 80 percent said they no longer feel threatened by the USSR. For forty years they felt threatened. How could things change so quickly in a fraction of that time? The press, not to be outdone by these waves of adulation, celebrated the new detente with exuberant raptures of relief. *The Washington Post*'s David Broder wrote of Gorbachev, "Not since John Kennedy lifted the hearts of West Berliners and made his face and name a symbol of hope in remote villages along the Amazon has there been a secular world figure of these dimensions."

A *New York Times* editorial gushed, "Imagine that an alien spaceship approached earth and sent the message, 'Take me to your leader.' Who would that be? Without doubt, Mikhail Sergeyevich Gorbachev."

Is there any justification for this sudden flowering of extravagant praise and goodwill? Perhaps. Perhaps not. The only way to judge is to recall some recent history. For Gorbachev is simply the latest in a long line of reformers that reaches to the beginning of the Soviet state. Whatever else Gorbachev's reforms may be — daring, deceptive, historic, tentative — they are certainly not new.

Lenin's Reform Movement

The first reform movement, in fact, was undertaken by the Soviet Union's founding father, V. I. Lenin. In the early 1920s, Lenin was faced with economic chaos brought on by years of revolution and civil war. Industry was producing next to nothing. There was no food in the cities. As many as three million people may have died from hunger in the winter of 1921–22. In Lenin's own words, "tens and hundreds of thousands of disbanded soldiers" were becoming bandits.[1]

Lenin's solution came to be known as the New Economic Policy (NEP). In violation of strict Marxist theory, he restored private ownership of small- and medium-sized businesses. And he allowed family farms to sell their surplus on the open market (The Chinese government did much the same before the crackdown on pro-democracy students in Beijing's Tiananmen Square in June 1989).

In addition, Lenin actively tried to lure Western industry into reconstructing the Soviet economy by appealing to what he called "their thirst for profit." Joseph Stalin later boasted that two-thirds of all industrial enterprises in the Soviet Union had been built in this period with United States help or technical assistance.

All the while, however, Lenin never allowed the dictatorial powers of the Communist party to be threatened or even questioned. The party retained strict control over what he called the "commanding heights" of the economy — large industry, mines, and banks.

The success of the NEP was phenomenal. The Soviet Union both avoided economic collapse and rebuilt some of its industrial base. But it was quickly followed by the grotesque brutality of Joseph Stalin, who undid Lenin's limited reforms and then executed the wealthier peasants who had benefitted from them.

Khrushchev's Thaw

It was Stalin's terror that gave birth to Russia's second great reformer, Nikita Khrushchev. His reform policy came to be known as the Thaw, beginning in 1956 with his denunciation of Stalin. Beriya, Stalin's sadistic head of the secret police, was executed for his crimes. Millions were released from labor camps. State censorship was relaxed—to the point that Aleksandr Solzhenitsyn's *One Day in the Life of Ivan Denisovich,* a stinging indictment of Stalin's system of gulags, was published with Khrushchev's approval.

But Nikita Khrushchev's foreign policy was anything but conciliatory. He gave active support to communist revolutionaries engaged in national "wars of liberation." And his style was openly confrontational—leading, in one instance, to the Cuban missile crisis.

Khrushchev's and Lenin's reform movements differed in detail, but they share three essential principles. Each was born, not out of the idealism of its leader, but out of simple economic or political need. Each tried to save the existing Soviet political and economic system, with all its traditional military objectives, not to change it fundamentally. And each was followed by a return to more strictly imposed repression.

Gorbachev's Reform: Principles

Do these principles set the limits of Gorbachev's reforms? It is impossible to be sure, but Gorbachev has been shaped by the goals and strategies of these earlier movements and for all of the talk of his "reforms," not one reform is irreversible. Remember Tiananmen Square in which several years of "reform" under Deng Xiaoping were obliterated in one bloody June night.

As a local party official, Gorbachev learned from Khrushchev's "Thaw" first-hand—particularly the necessity of consolidating unquestioned personal power. And he has often claimed, "These days we turn ever more often to the last works of Lenin, to his New Economic Policy, and we strive to extract from those ideas all the valuable elements we require today."[2]

In Gorbachev's case, like Lenin's, he has been forced into economic reform and military reductions by simple economic necessity, not some sort of idealism. The Soviet Union now spends about 20 percent of its gross national product on its military—three times the proportion of the United States. And, in the process, it has run up a $165 billion national debt.

But it is chronically short on hard cash. In 1987 the Soviet Union earned only $35 billion abroad in sound money—about half what General Motors takes in each year in sales.

Like many empires of the past, it also has begun to suffer from imperial overstretch, throwing good money after bad (if the Soviet ruble can be said to be good given its worthlessness in the international monetary system) to prop up bankrupt client states—$2 billion a year to Vietnam, $1.5 billion to Angola, $1 billion to Nicaragua, $5 billion, or $14 million a day to keep Cuba afloat. And all this money is spent on weapons and aid while Soviet citizens wait in long lines for basic necessities, some of which, like toilet paper, are rapidly becoming luxuries. One Soviet newspaper reported, "The general view in the Soviet Union is that conditions of life have not been bad for twenty years."[3]

As the world spins toward the twenty-first century, large sections of the Soviet Union have yet to march into the nineteenth century. One out of every six hospitals in the USSR has no running water. Thirty percent have no sewage systems. And life expectancy for males in the Soviet Union is actually declining, one of the few places in the world where this is the case.

Soviet citizens must work ten to twelve times as long as their American counterparts in order to buy the same amount of meat; ten to fifteen times the work for the same number of eggs; eighteen to twenty-five times the work for fresh fruit. They have six to ten times less living space than the average American. And, given the drab poverty of Soviet society (and here I am talking not only about the economic variety, but the spiritual, social, and moral as well), it is perhaps understandable that they spend 15 percent of their yearly income on alcohol.

So despondent are Soviet citizens over their lot that a prominent reform of the Gorbachev era, a campaign to reduce the consumption of vodka by shortening the hours of liquor stores and conducting anti-drinking campaigns in the Soviet press, failed miserably. Drinking, and the social costs associated with it, continue unabated.

The Soviet Union has been aptly called a third world nation with first world weapons. And this combination of economic backwardness and massive military expenditure could not be maintained for long. Gorbachev's reforms are an admission of economic failure—an acknowledgment that changes are necessary if the Soviets are to remain a superpower.

Second, it is also clear that Gorbachev's reforms, like those that came before, are intended to save the Soviet system and its objectives, not to replace that system or its objectives. Gorbachev has spoken only vaguely about lessening confrontation around the world, but when the American Congress cut off aid to the anti-Sandinista forces in Nicaragua, Soviet aid continued as before. And, while it is true that the Soviets pulled out of Afghanistan, their reasons had nothing to do with peacemaking. They were compelled to leave by the resolve of the Mujahedin fighters who were the recipients of American economic and military aid. That Congress failed to see the connection between Afghanistan and Nicaragua is a continuing mystery.

Perestroika **and** *Glasnost*

There are two distinct parts of Gorbachev's reforms, neither of which are as ground-breaking as they might appear. The first is *perestroika,* or restructuring—encouragement of small-scale free enterprise as an incentive to production. It's an idea as old as Lenin's New Economic Policy. And then, as now, it was intended as a set of reforms within socialism to save socialism, not an attempt to change the system wholesale.

Again like Lenin, Gorbachev has ensured that the role of the Communist party remains primary. He argued, in fact, during the July 1988 Party Congress that "the resolution of the tasks of restructuring requires enhancement of the party's leading role."[4]

The second part of Gorbachev's reform movement is *glasnost* or openness—a new tolerance for criticism and free expression. And here the results have been more dramatic. Art, literature, political dissent, even religious expression, have seen some restrictions lifted.

But *glasnost* is still a gift from the Kremlin, specifically Gorbachev. Unlike the American system in which "all Men are created equal and are endowed by their Creator with certain unalienable rights," what the Soviet leader gives, he or his successor can take away.

Jean-Francois Revel, a prominent French political commentator, argues, "Today's *glasnost,* like yesterday's Thaw, is a gift from on high. It is an instrument through which the General Secretary can consolidate his own power by using the press to indict and little by little, eliminate his predecessor's men."[5] Natan Sharansky, who spent nine years as a Soviet political prisoner, contends, "*Glasnost* is not a form of freedom. It's just a new set of instructions on what is and isn't permitted."[6]

Whatever the merits of *perestroika* and *glasnost,* these reforms have not changed the nature of the Soviet military threat. As Europe looks to the East, it sees a Soviet army with more divisions in East Germany than in the entire U.S. Army, and more divisions in Czechoslovakia than there are U.S. divisions in all of Europe. Each Soviet division has forward-deployed mobile bridging equipment that is useful only for offense. Under Gorbachev, some older weapons have been retired. But they have largely been replaced by tanks and artillery of more advanced technology.

After Reforms, What?

The final historical principle of Soviet reform is the predictable progression from reform to repression. And with Gorbachev the jury is still out. Still, we are not without some disturbing signs. When the veteran Soviet diplomat, the late Andrei Gromyko, nominated Gorbachev for the General Secretaryship, he warned that the new leader has a "broad smile but teeth of steel." Gorbachev hasn't bitten down hard with these teeth, but if the pattern of traditional reform holds, he, or his successor, will eventually do so.

Many, including both his supporters and critics, see Gorbachev's decision to use the Red Army to quell Armenian unrest in early 1988 (and his implied threats to do the same to end a coal miner's strike in the summer of 1989) as evidence that he is already resorting to force to set the limits of reform. The Kremlin's stricter laws on political demonstrations introduced in 1988 seem to support this view as well.

Gorbachev continues to support brutal client states like North Korea, Cuba, Ethiopia, and Nicaragua which make use of mass terror as an instrument of policy. And his direction of the last stages of the war in Afghanistan violated every civilized standard. He has left that nation a legacy of scorched earth, contaminated wells, poisoned food supplies, and millions of hidden mines, some disguised as toys, that will continue to maim Afghan children for generations.

Some would represent Mikhail Gorbachev as a genuine social reformer — less interested in ideology than in easing the dingy lot of the average Soviet worker — a sort of communist Franklin Roosevelt.

It is a pleasing, as well as a seductive, prospect. All our most pressing political and military problems are solved simply and dramatically, by our enemy ceasing to be our enemy.

But it is also the least plausible of several more disturbing alternatives. We would do well to remember the lessons of past Soviet reform — cynical cycles of liberalization and repression. The exception in Grenada was due to American resolve, not communist cold feet.

But the best evidence of his intentions comes from Gorbachev himself. In the closing lines of his speech commemorating the seventieth anniversary of the Bolshevik coup of the legitimate Russian Revolution, he said, "In October, 1917, we parted with the old world, rejecting it once and for all. We are moving toward a new world, the world of communism. We shall never turn off that road."[7]

Khrushchev said much the same thing: "Do not believe we have forgotten Marx, Engels, and Lenin," he said. "They will not be forgotten until shrimp learn to sing."

The last shrimp I ate lay mute on my plate.

We must now decide whether to take Gorbachev (and Khrushchev) at their words or risk seducing ourselves by wishing upon a star instead of grounding our thinking in the cold, hard realities of past behavior.

AT ISSUE

EASTERN EUROPE

LIFE WITHOUT
THE RED MENACE

THE WARM WINDS blowing across U.S.-Soviet relations are said by some to have ended the Cold War. Therefore, reasons one journalist, why shouldn't reporters begin to re-think the way they cover the formerly evil empire?

In a remarkable essay in the January 1989 issue of *The Quill*, a publication of the Sigma Delta Chi professional journalism fraternity, the foreign editor of *The Baltimore Sun*, Richard O'Mara, suggests that "pack journalism" brought on by the "competitive nature of our business," rather than criminal Soviet behavior of the past seven decades, has defined the content and character of American press coverage of the Soviet Union.

O'Mara accepts at face value—with only occasional disclaimers ("of course, it is not written in stone that *glasnost* will continue unimpeded, or that Gorbachev's *perestroika* will succeed")—the public pronouncements of various Soviet officials that a new day has dawned along the Moscow River.

Journalists were trapped into covering the Cold War and even contributing to it, argues O'Mara, because we are easily manipulated; we are conformists: "It is extremely difficult for an individual, or an individual newspaper or magazine, to resist the engines of propaganda that Washington commands."

So, Washington runs a propaganda engine and pronouncements from Moscow are to be believed? This is Orwellian newthink in full flower. O'Mara sees the history of Soviet-American conflict not in geopolitical or ideological terms, but rather as William Randolph Hearst hype designed to sell newspapers. This is all a misunderstanding to which the American (but not the Soviet) press has contributed and from which it must now withdraw.

Yes, we were all in it just for the money, suggests O'Mara, "Livelihoods are linked to the doctrine of perpetual conflict between the superpowers." And it will be difficult to change, he asserts, because "jobs would be threatened by more benign interpretations of Soviet intentions. Funding for academics, consultants, right-wing politicians and their advisers and their think tanks might dry up."

O'Mara does not suggest that news bureaus be shut, just that journalists turn their eyes in another direction.

O'Mara's article is proof that the Soviets are on the right track in their attempt to deplete America's resolve to resist any challenges to the principles of freedom and democracy. Whatever else the Soviets may have in mind with their new public relations effort, they would clearly relish a loss of American will.

This is not the first time we have heard from the press encouraging us to trust the Soviets. Walter Duranty of *The New York Times* parroted the Soviet line during Stalin's regime. As British journalist Malcolm Muggeridge later wrote,

> This was not because the *Times* was deceived. Rather, because it wanted to be deceived, and Duranty provided the requisite deception material. Since his time there have been a whole succession of others fulfilling the same role — in Cuba, in Vietnam, in Latin America. It is an addiction, and in such cases there is never any lack of hands to push in the needle and give the fix. Just as the intelligentsia have been foremost in the struggle to abolish intelligence, so the great organs of capitalism like *The New York Times* have spared no expense to ensure that capitalism will not survive.

A far better observer of Soviet intentions is Soviet writer Andrei Sinyavsky, who was recently quoted concerning the supposed change in his country: "It's not that I don't believe in it; it's that I don't trust it."

Perhaps journalism would benefit more from the thoughts of a seasoned observer like Sinyavsky than a misguided thinker like O'Mara.

AT ISSUE

EASTERN EUROPE

GOD AND MAN IN RUSSIA

W HEN THE VICAR of the former
"evil empire" met the "Vicar of Christ" in the Vatican last week, what
he said concerning religion would have been ideological heresy to Lenin
and all the other Soviet leaders who followed him.

Mikhail Gorbachev told Pope John Paul II, "We have changed our
attitude on some matters, such as religion. . . . Now we not only proceed
from the assumption that no one should interfere in matters of the
individual's conscience, we also say that the moral values that religion
generated and embodied for centuries can help in the work of renewal in
our country, too."

These remarks are nearly verbatim what evangelist Billy Graham
told several high-ranking Soviet officials during his 1987 visit to Moscow. It appears that Gorbachev, whether for pragmatic or other reasons,
has become a believer in religion's capacity for motivating the Soviet
people to pull their country out of its economic doldrums.

Karl Marx's dictum that "Religion is the opium of the people" became a fixation for Joseph Stalin, who included many religious believers
among the 60 million Soviet citizens Aleksandr Solzhenitsyn estimates
the dictator slaughtered. Jews, Evangelical Baptists, Pentacostalists, and
other believers in a power higher than the state have long been targeted
by the Kremlin as worthy of special persecution, harassment, prison, and
death. Beginning with Lenin and through modern times, the Soviet Constitution and the Articles of the Russian Criminal Code have been used

to control the spread of religion in the Soviet Union. Kent R. Hill, executive director of The Institute on Religion and Democracy, reprints them in his timely new book, *The Puzzle of the Soviet Church.*

Look for instance at Article 142 of the criminal code, which says, "Violation of the laws on the separation of church and state and of school and church . . . is punishable by correctional tasks for a period not exceeding one year or by a fine not exceeding 50 rubles." Subsequent offenses lead to stiffer penalties.

Under this article, it is an offense to organize any activity of any unregistered church and teach religion to children, except one's own. Baptist Pastor Georgi Vins was sentenced to prison, where he nearly died, for not registering with the state and for printing illegal religious literature. In a deal worked out by President Carter a decade ago, Vins was given his freedom in a swap for some Soviet spies.

Then there is Article 227: "Infringement of the person and rights of citizens under the guise of performing religious rituals." Introduced in 1959, it was initially directed mainly at Pentacostals. But as Michael Bourdeux has written in his *May One Believe — in Russia?*: "It was soon also applied to Baptists who left the officially recognized church and has been applied to Christians of almost all denominations and even to Buddhists. The essential features are 'causing harm to health (frequently states to result from speaking in tongues by Pentacostals)' and 'inciting citizens to refuse to do social activity,' for example, urging members not to take part in secular cultural activities."

Apparently the appeals of Soviet religious rights activist Gleb Yakunin and Billy Graham for greater religious freedom have moved Gorbachev. The Soviet president seems to recognize what Yakunin said last year: "Religion is like salt that protects humanity from decomposition and disintegration. Any attempt to banish it from social life invariably leads to a degradation of society."

But before Gorbachev's promises of more religious freedom can be taken seriously, he must push for repeal of Article 142 and Article 227 and the dozens of others that have been used against religious believers.

As Kent Hill writes in his book, "Before religion can ever be secure, antireligious ideology must be publicly and firmly renounced as incompatible with a progressive, socially just, modern Soviet State. This means nothing less than a conscious and public departure from the convictions of the German and Russian founders of Marxist communism."

Nothing less will produce the zeal Gorbachev seeks for rebuilding his economically and spiritually broken nation.

AT ISSUE

EASTERN EUROPE

FREEDOM AND BONDAGE IN EASTERN EUROPE

NOT LONG AFTER the dominoes began falling in Eastern Europe, *Playboy* magazine bought a full-page ad in *The New York Times* to announce that it had become the first "American consumer magazine" to be published in Hungarian. *Playboy* said it was not surprised "since we're the magazine that led a social revolution in America by standing for personal, political, and economic freedom." The headline on the ad read "Exporting The American Dream."

More like an American nightmare, since many of those who embraced the *Playboy* philosophy of "if it feels good, do it" have suffered broken marriages, unwanted pregnancies, abortion, and AIDS.

If Eastern Europe thought communism was a difficult yoke to bear, wait until it gets a sample of Western-style hedonism. Already the missionaries of decadence are at work.

East Germany, having torn down parts of the hated Berlin Wall, now appears ready to redefine "naked aggression." The first East German Playmate of the Month is Anja Kossak, who reveals among other things in the magazine's German-language January issue how difficult she has found lovemaking in the tiny Trabant automobile. The magazine had been banned under the former dictator, Erich Honecker.

Then Romanians, who gained their freedom in a horrible bloodbath, authorized the shedding of other innocent blood by legalizing abortion on demand. It had been a jailable offense under late dictator Nicolae Ceausescu, though his motives for banning the procedure were not pure.

Lenin believed that the sole function of a revolutionary was to tear down the existing structure with no thought to what might replace it. That can produce one of two results: anarchy or dictatorship. The cycles of history are full of examples of nations that have emancipated themselves from dictatorships to win their freedom, only to move without an anchor or set of fixed social absolutes into a regressive spiral that sucked them into materialism and decadence and back into bondage.

Freedom may have been "1989's Word of the Year," as William Safire writes, but freedom sometimes arrives accompanied by an ugly relative called license. Without a set of moral standards, the wind of freedom could quickly become a whirlwind of moral anarchy.

It is here that the persecuted Christians of Eastern Europe can and must be of help. While there were different brands of communism, the Communists were united in their hatred for and persecution of Christianity. Still, while atheism flourished, so did the underground churches. Now the test will be whether Christian churches, refined through persecution, have the courage to build a foundation that will fill the moral, economic, and political vacuum left by communism's demise.

American churches, so many grown fat, lazy, and prosperous, should shake off their complacency and begin a "Marshall Plan" of their own, sending food, fuel, and other necessities to Eastern Europe. Various civic groups, private charities, and the Peace Corps could also assist.

William Middendorf, former U.S. ambassador to the European Economic Community, believes that Eastern Europe's "honeymoon period" will last from six months to a year. Then people will begin complaining about the lack of fundamental needs.

"These countries must go all the way to full private property rights and a capitalist economic system, just as West German Chancellor Werner Erhard did in 1946, or their experiment will fail," Middendorf told me. "You can't have political pluralism without economic pluralism."

Middendorf said that if American churches and other charitable groups assist Eastern Europe with their basic needs in the short term, it will give those who want to lead Eastern Europe into a brighter political and economic future more time to discover the superiority of capitalism and the dangers inherent in an alloy of socialism and capitalism.

The new Czechoslovakian president, Vaclav Havel, seems to have grasped his nation's most fundamental need in a New Year's Day address: ". . . we live in a spoiled environment. We have become morally ill because we are used to saying one thing and thinking another. We have learned not to believe in anything, not to care about each other, to worry only about ourselves. The concepts of love, friendship, mercy, humility, or forgiveness have lost their depths and dimension, and for many of us they represent only some sort of psychological curiosity or they appear as long-lost wanderers from faraway times, somewhat ludicrous in the era of computers and spaceships."

Surely, as Czechoslovakia and the rest of Eastern Europe struggle with matters of the spirit, Americans could do better than to make *Playboy* and Pepsi Cola among their primary exports. If we fail to help meet Eastern Europe's deeper needs, as well as its need for food and fuel, the euphoria there and here will be short-lived.

AT ISSUE

EASTERN EUROPE

THE MAN OF THE DECADE

TIME MAGAZINE has named Soviet President Mikhail Gorbachev its "Man of the Decade." In gushing tones, suitable for the adulation due a newly elected Pope, *Time*'s Strobe Talbott writes, "Gorbachev is helping the West by showing that the Soviet threat isn't what it used to be — and, what's more, that it never was." What a short memory he has. Whose troops and tanks and foreign military assistance have been used since World War II to subjugate people and nations under the hammer and sickle?

Talbott also elevates Gorbachev to a kind of political messiah when he writes, "So far, Gorbachev has had a near monopoly on the promulgation of bold ideas." Another *Time* editor goes even further: "Gorbachev has transformed the world."

Time has picked the wrong person. The credit for *perestroika* and *glasnost,* the credit for what has occurred in Eastern Europe, the credit for the destruction of the Berlin Wall and the toppling of communist regimes right up to the borders of the Soviet Union should not go to the "Man of the Decade," Mikhail Gorbachev, but to Ronald Reagan.

Without Reagan's steadfast determination to rebuild America's defenses, without Reagan's vigorous rhetoric and consistent opposition to communism, without Reagan's tremendous election victories, demonstrating strong support from Americans, it's inconceivable that President Gorbachev would even have allowed the changes for which he is now praised as having initiated. One has to ignore a lot of recent history to pass over Ronald Reagan for recognition as the architect of the world's reconstruction. He was relentless in his denunciation of communism. In a 1983 speech to the National Association of Evangelicals (the famous "evil empire" address), Reagan made a prediction that was remarkably accurate: "I believe that communism is another sad, bizarre chapter in human history whose last pages even now are being written. I believe this because the source of our strength in the quest for human freedom is not material but spiritual, and because it knows no limitation, it must terrify and ultimately triumph over those who would enslave their fellow man."

He prophesied that the "march of freedom and democracy will leave Marxism-Leninism on the ash heap of history as it has left other tyrannies which stifle the freedom and muzzle the self-expression of the people."

There is no comparable soaring rhetoric from the "Man of the Decade."

In fact, can anyone doubt that Gorbachev's actions during the 1980s were simply a response to an agenda set by Reagan? It was Reagan who, in 1983, ordered the liberation of Grenada, showing that the U.S. would no longer be a patsy for communist expansion around the world. Two years later Reagan refused to panic when the Soviets walked out of negotiations on intermediate range missiles, taking a stand that led to eventual completion of a treaty. Reagan backed Radio Marti to "promote the cause of freedom in Cuba," and — against the advice of the State Department — ordered a reduction in the number of Soviet "diplomats" at its U.N. mission to reduce the potential for spying.

He renounced the SALT II treaty after several major violations by the Soviets. And numerous times he challenged Gorbachev to tear down the Berlin Wall.

Reagan didn't back down when a 1983 "peacenik" offensive threatened to block the introduction of U.S. cruise missiles at England's Greenham Common air base and the first battery of Pershing IIs in West Germany. Nor did he back down when critics repeatedly attacked his commitment to the Strategic Defense Initiative. And when most other world leaders practiced a policy of appeasement toward terrorism, Reagan ordered an attack on Libyan leader Moammar Kadafi.

In one of his most remarkable addresses, at Moscow State University in May 1988, Reagan spoke of a technological revolution sweeping the planet, but he said that the key to progress was freedom, "freedom of thought, freedom of information, freedom of communication." He said, "the growth of democracy has become one of the most important political movements of our age."

There was no better preacher of freedom than Ronald Reagan, who stood under a huge likeness of Lenin at Moscow State and told students and faculty, "Your generation is living in one of the most exciting, hopeful times in Soviet history. It is a time when the first breath of freedom stirs in the air, and the heart beats to the accelerated rhythm of hope, when the accumulated spiritual energies of a long silence yearn to break free."

Less than six months after that speech those energies began to be unleashed in Eastern Europe. They may soon sweep into the Soviet Union. Mikhail Gorbachev may be *allowing* this to happen, but it was Ronald Reagan who *made* it happen.

In 1949, *Time* named Winston Churchill "Man of the Half-Century." The magazine ought to name Reagan the man of *this* half-century. Whether it does or not, history will so regard him.

AT ISSUE

THE POLICY

U.S. FOREIGN POLICY

W HEN REPORTERS asked his opin-
ion of events in Europe, President Warren Harding, whose interests were
centered more on the bedroom than the Cabinet room, thought a few
moments, and replied, "I don't know anything about this European
stuff."[1]

It is an attitude that has been more common among Americans than
our recently re-discovered spirit of globalism. Protected by vast oceans
on our East and West and resentful of European "entanglements," isolation, a fancy word for studied indifference, comes to most Americans
naturally.

Isolation

As late as the mid-1920s, the State Department had a staff of just six
hundred people, supported by a budget of only $2 million. (In 1990, there
were 24,406 employees and the Department's budget had ballooned to
more than two billion, 800 million dollars.) In the 1920s, there simply
was not much need to talk to a world about which we cared little.

That indifference was often accompanied by an extraordinary na-
ivete. Americans generally believed they could clean up the European
mess in short order and quickly go back to minding their own business
and businesses. Calvin Coolidge observed, "The business of America is
business." The order of the day was idealism, passivity, and neutrality.

On July 27, 1928, the United States signed the Kellogg-Briand pact—a long-forgotten treaty that ceremoniously banned offensive war forever. The Secretary of State, Frank Kellogg, received the Nobel Peace Prize in 1929 for his idea. By 1934 sixty-four nations had signed the document. A decade later, most of the signatories were at war.

In 1944 Patrick Hurley, Franklin Roosevelt's personal representative in China, reported that Mao Zedong was an agrarian populist, "The only difference between Chinese Communists and Oklahoma Republicans is that Oklahoma Republicans aren't armed."[2]

In January 1938 congressional isolationists brought to a vote a constitutional amendment that would only allow the United States to pursue war if it were approved by a national referendum. They failed only after an extraordinary appeal directly from President Roosevelt.

Much, if not most, isolationist sentiment came from conservatives. Groups like "America First" and newspapers such as The Chicago Tribune preached a doctrine of withdrawal into a fortress America.

But before World War I ("the war to end all wars"), there was a long tradition of left isolationism as well, which has been reborn in the post-Vietnam era. Socialist Norman Thomas argued that the cost of foreign commitments would prevent economic reconstruction at home. Progressives like William Borah and Robert LaFollette opposed foreign involvement on principle. Both Woodrow Wilson and Franklin Roosevelt were elected on promises of staying out of European conflicts. Left and right isolationism were the American mainstream.

Internationalism

This changed with the two world wars. Americans found that this "European stuff" snuffed out lives and innocence in the trenches and gas clouds of the Great War. It introduced us to fascism and genocide just twenty years later. Pearl Harbor shocked America out of indifference. Many, like isolationist Arthur Vandenberg, turned internationalist when they saw London fall under German V-rocket attacks in 1944. "How can there be any immunity or isolation when men can devise weapons like that?" asked Vandenberg.[3]

This new internationalism met with success and influence at very little cost. World War I cost the United States one-tenth of one percent of its population in war-related deaths. Great Britain lost nearly that figure between 7 A.M. and 7 P.M. on July 1, 1916 at the Battle of the Somme. In World War II, the United States lost one-quarter of one percent of its population, suffering just four civilian deaths from home-front bombing. (A Japanese balloon bomb, launched from a submarine, exploded at an Oregon picnic.) The Soviet Union lost at least 8 percent of its population. American isolationism was submerged by success. But after World War II there were signs it would reemerge. The Soviet threat seemed every bit as menacing as the defeated Nazis. Yet popular pressure forced a reduction in the size of the American military from eleven million men to just one million.

In view of the contemporary isolationist spirit exhibited by most liberal Democrats, it was interesting to note that an unlikely champion stood in the way of this retrenchment—Harry Truman. On March 12, 1947, what George Will calls "the most important date in postwar history,"[4] Truman appeared before the Congress to request $400 million in emergency military and economic aid to Greece and Turkey, both under communist threat. "I believe," said Truman, "it must be the policy of the United States to support free people who are resisting attempted subjugation by armed minorities or by outside pressure."[5]

The Truman Doctrine and the whole postwar policy of containment reached its apogee with John F. Kennedy, the last of the national non-isolationist Democrats. Kennedy's inaugural address, with its call for sacrifice anywhere, anytime in the "long twilight struggle" for human freedom, expressed a new consensus on America's place in the world. It was activist, interventionist, and strident—just the opposite of America's traditional fortress mentality.

This was the legacy of the Democratic Party. Republicans, at first, resisted this new internationalism. Soon, they followed along. But it was Democrats who led. "The (Democratic) Party," writes George Will, "had been the principal foe of the principal evil of our century—totalitarianism. The party was characterized by Wilson's opposition to Lenin, Roosevelt's to Hitler, Truman's to Stalin, Kennedy's to Castro, Kennedy's and Johnson's to Asian communism. Democrats defined and waged the Cold War and did it well."[6]

The hard evidence was Kennedy's sending of 16,000 troops to Vietnam to fight communism. Vietnam ended up destroying Lyndon Johnson's presidency, as the body count mounted in interminable combat. But this failure did more than that. It destroyed the nation's bipartisan commitment to internationalism.

America had taken the international stage in the world wars with great effect and little sacrifice. In the cause of idealism and anti-communism, it violated a long American tradition that knew little of the world and cared even less. But the Cold War, culminating in Vietnam, gradually re-awakened this tendency. "With World War II," writes Charles Krauthammer, "both left and right isolationism went into eclipse, not to reemerge until Vietnam."[7] It found explicit form in the isolationist vision of George McGovern's "Come Home America" campaign in 1972. And it has begun to influence both the political Left and political Right once again.

Liberal Isolationism

The McGovern campaign changed the ground rules of international relations for Democrats. "Left isolationism," comments Krauthammer, "has become the ideology of the Democratic party, not of its 'McGovernite' fringes but of its mainstream."[8] It has become difficult at times to recognize the party of Roosevelt and Kennedy.

"In 1984," comments George Will, "Gary Hart and Walter Mondale engaged in a bidding war to see who could propose the most complete and rapid withdrawal from the most places, with special reference to Central America."[9] The 1984 Democratic platform contained ten references to "multilateralism"—an increasingly popular code word for inaction and isolation. It seems clear that if a nation can only act if its allies act, the most timid ally is given an absolute vote on any action.

After the invasion of Grenada (the Reagan Administration called it a "rescue" because of the intent of rescuing medical students on the island), New York Senator Daniel Moynihan objected, "You don't bring democracy at the point of a bayonet."[10]

"That idea," writes Charles Krauthammer, "would come as a surprise to the Germans and Japanese" (and now the Grenadians and Panamanians, too), "the beneficiaries of an earlier Democratic internationalism that defined itself precisely by its insistence on the relationship between democracy and bayonets."[11]

Senator John Glenn has talked of Democratic colleagues that "shrink from even legitimate uses of force."[12]

The chief legislative accomplishment of the new liberal isolationism came in 1973 with the War Powers Act. The act, which many believe to be an unconstitutional infringement upon the powers of the President as commander-in-chief of the nation's armed forces, states that when the American military is used, or "where imminent involvement in hostilities is clearly indicated by circumstances," the President is required within forty-eight hours to report to Congress the "circumstances necessitating" his act, the "constitutional and legislative authority" for it, and the "estimated scope and duration" of it. Within sixty days, the deployment must end if Congress refuses to approve it.

This is a novel interpretation of the President's power as commander-in-chief, flying in the face of hundreds of presidential actions, from the earliest days of the nation. George Will argues, "Either Congress was wrong in its 1973 venture into constitutional construction, or most Presidents — including all the liberal pinups, from Teddy Roosevelt to Woodrow Wilson through FDR and JFK — have behaved unconstitutionally."[13]

Liberal isolationism has taken control of a political party. Right isolationism, as yet, has not. But it has grown in strength. Commentators like Patrick Buchanan call for a withdrawal of American troops from Europe. Intellectuals like Irving Kristol make the case for abandoning European military commitments. A conservative Democrat, Sam Nunn of Georgia, is the leader of efforts to cut U.S. troop strength in Europe. Some commentators have seen in the Strategic Defense Initiative (or "Star Wars") the promise of an America that relies exclusively on its own defense — the traditional isolationism of the Right. "Although right isolationists draw different lines," Charles Krauthammer argues, "the sentiment animating their efforts is the same: a sense that America has let itself be drawn into commitments that serve not its interests but that of others. From Washington's Farewell Address on, that sentiment has always animated classical isolationism. . . . Chastened by the interwar failure of the European system, it came to accept that American interests could best be served through American-dominated internationalist vehicles. That domination now ended, many conservatives want out. They want to redraw the lines of the American sphere, and withdraw to its unencumbered defense."[14]

Left and right isolationism could well have economic and political benefits. Following the remarkable developments in Eastern Europe at the end of 1989, liberals and conservatives began talking of a "peace dividend" for the treasury. And it is certainly consistent with the mainstream of America's approach to the world, interrupted only by a short period of crusading interventionism from the 1940s to the 1960s.

But there seem to be costs as well. One conservative advocate of the fortress America concept, Robert Tucker, in his book, *New Isolationism,* admits, "the price of a new isolationism is that America would have to abandon its aspirations to an order that has become synonymous with the nation's vision of its role in the world." He adds, "Isolationism is opposed, among other reasons, because it is equated with indifference to the fate of others. . . . It undoubtedly is and no useful purpose is served by evasiveness on this point."[15]

Internationalism was thrust upon America, but its legacy has been an enduring contribution to freedom. It was tested in Germany, Japan and Korea, as American soldiers and American foreign policy fought vicious tyrannies. It was sustained by an anti-communism that contained Soviet aggression for decades. It is the principle, perhaps the only explanation, for the liberty of millions. Whatever Mikhail Gorbachev is and whatever the motives behind his *perestroika,* surely it must be clear to most people that he is not a born-again Democrat. Had America not been involved in the world, which is her right as well as her privilege, Soviet communism would not be in retreat, but advancing everywhere on the planet.

"To disengage in the service of a narrow nationalism," concludes Krauthammer, "is a fine foreign policy for a minor regional power, which the United States once was and which, say, Canada or Sweden now are. For America today, it is a betrayal of its idea of itself. Most of all, it seems a curious application of American conservatism, which usually holds liberty to be the highest of political values. Does that idea now stop at the nation's shores?"[16]

AT ISSUE

THE POLICY

T H I R T Y - N I N E

FOREIGN POLICY EXPERTS

THE TWO MEN SITTING next to me on the flight from Texas to Washington were conversing about the Soviet Union and President Reagan's Strategic Defense Initiative (SDI). They were Senate staff members, heading home after a week of visits to SDI research sites.

As I joined the conversation, one of the men began talking about the "new wind" he thinks is blowing in the Soviet Union and how "different" Mikhail Gorbachev is from his predecessors. The other man asserted that "communism is not genetic" and that it can change.

I asked them if they had ever been to the Soviet Union. Neither had. Had either of them ever read the works of Lenin? No.

"How is it, then," I asked, "that you know so much about Gorbachev and about communism?" Their reply was not unlike that of Jiminy Crickett, who sang, "When you wish upon a star your dreams come true." This is what passes for serious foreign policy analysis in some congressional quarters these days.

Two men with far better understanding of the world have just published their own thoughts about Gorbachev that should be must reading for all Americans, especially every member of Congress.

Former President Richard Nixon, in his new book, *1999: Victory Without War,* gives the clearest, most concise, and highly readable critique of the Soviet Union under Gorbachev that I have ever read. And the former Jewish refusenik, Natan Sharansky, has made an equally important contribution in the March 1989 issue of *Commentary* magazine.

In his book, Nixon has again demonstrated an insight into foreign affairs that is unsurpassed. About the Soviet leader's ability to captivate the public and the press, Nixon says, "If we mistake a change in style of leadership for a change in Soviet international goals, Gorbachev may capture the rest of the West as well.

"The beginning of the Gorbachev era does not represent the end of the rivalry between the two superpowers. Rather, it represents the beginning of a dangerous, challenging new stage of the struggle."

Nixon says it is "fatuous nonsense" to believe that Gorbachev's neatly tailored suits, refined manners, attractive wife, and smooth touch with reporters reveal a man far different from his cold-blooded Soviet predecessors.

Not stopping at hard-hitting analysis, Nixon goes beyond criticisms to a six-point proposal for engaging the Soviets around the world. As Congress moves to further restrict the president's ability to conduct covert operations, Nixon says, ". . . it would be a fatal mistake for the United States to renounce covert action as a foreign policy instrument, because the Soviets continue to exploit covert operations to arm insurgencies, finance Communist and other leftist parties, disseminate disinformation, train international terrorists, and assassinate opponents." In his *Commentary* article, Sharansky states flatly that "*glasnost* is not a form of freedom. It's just a new set of instructions on what is and isn't permitted."

Sharansky, who has earned his right to be heard after spending nine years in Soviet prisons and labor camps for the "crime" of calling on the Soviet leadership to live up to the Helsinki accords, makes these points: Gorbachev's reforms will not lead to the democratization of Soviet society or to true pluralism; *perestroika* will never fully succeed, and any success it achieves will depend on Western cooperation; the Soviets have finally awakened to the value of the "television smile, a modulated voice, and an amicable appearance as far more effective than bullying and threats" and immeasurably more important than substance in shaping public opinion; despite their dire economic conditions, the Soviets have not diminished their military budget or aid to client states; there has been no letup in anti-American propaganda, including continued allegations that AIDS was created as a biological warfare weapon and that the CIA murdered the 918 Jim Jones cultists to prevent them from emigrating to the Soviet Union.

Richard Nixon and Natan Sharansky have contributed more realistic suggestions about how the United States ought to compete successfully with the Soviets in the world than any Administration official, and certainly any member of the increasingly isolationist Congress.

AT ISSUE

CENTRAL AMERICA

CENTRAL AMERICA

R EVOLUTIONARY TURMOIL is not a recent visitor to Latin America. In the first decade of this century, brutal warlords competed for power in nations across the region. Mexican disorder spilled over into the American Southwest, spread by Pancho Villa — a colorful revolutionary hero of whom the late historian Barbara Tuchman wrote, "On one occasion, angered by yells of a drunken soldier while he was being interviewed by an American journalist, Villa casually pulled his pistol and killed the man from the window, without interrupting the conversation."[1]

Lord Bryce, Britain's ambassador to the United States, warned President Wilson that "the best thing that can happen is to get as soon as possible a dictator who will keep order."[2] But Wilson responded with typical moral inflexibility: "I intend to teach the Latin American republics to elect good men."[3]

Unable to find enough "good men," Wilson was eventually forced to send the army into Mexico. But his insistence that the primary aim of his policy in the region was to spread democracy and prosperity has characterized American diplomacy ever since.

In the decades that have followed, his pledge has often rung hollow — particularly as Marines debarked from time to time to defend American interests and fight revolutionary brushfires in the region. But in the 1980s, suddenly and surprisingly, democracy appears on the march.

A coup in El Salvador in 1979, followed by elections in 1982, 1984, and 1985, has brought that nation progressive reforms. Guatemala has edged toward democracy with free elections. Costa Rica remains an outpost of stability and freedom. In 1986 Honduras inaugurated a new president, marking for the first time in more than fifty years that one Honduran elected civilian succeeded another as chief executive. Across Central America, old dictatorships and oligarchies have given way to infant democratic institutions.

There are some exceptions. Cuba remains an island prison, kept running only by continual infusion of Soviet aid. But even that may not last much longer. Soviet President Mikhail Gorbachev has told Fidel Castro to expect a reduction in Soviet assistance, which has been the primary source of income for Cuba's bankrupt economy. Panama, which for years festered as a drug dictatorship under Manuel Noriega, was liberated by American forces in December 1989. Noriega's capture and transfer to the United States for trial, was the second nation in the region delivered from bondage by an American president (Grenada was the first).

To the surprise of most "experts" and the press, which had called the election in favor of the Sandinistas, Nicaragua was offered its first real chance at democracy in decades when Violetta Chamorro trounced dictator Daniel Ortega in February 1990 elections.

Because the recent history of Nicaragua and its relations with the United States served as an example of the tension between the political and religious right and left wings, it is instructive to focus on one of the longest-running conflicts in American political history. It should be noted that as this is written, Ortega was still head of the Sandinista army and vowing to "rule from below" until he and his colleagues could regain control of the country. Given their violent revolutionary history, it should come as no surprise if Ortega attempts to undermine the Chamorro government.

The Debate over Nicaragua

During the decade-long debate over Nicaragua, views differed so dramatically that it was often difficult to imagine that debaters were dealing with the same facts.

For some, Nicaragua was the archetype of a petty communist dictatorship. For others, it embodied innovative social progress and a Christian preference for the poor. Catholic theologian Henri Nouwen observed, after a visit to Nicaragua,

> Some say, "What is happening is nationalism: a country trying to determine its own future." Others say, "No, it's internationalism: a country becoming the victim of Cuban-Soviet domination." Some say, "What you see in Nicaragua is the best example of a revolution in which Christian values are truly integrated." Others say, "No, it is a revolution based on atheistic principles and bent on the eradication of all religious belief."[4]

Nicaraguan history, in many ways, is the history of Central America in miniature—a story of disorder, rescue, and resentment. Before 1912 Nicaraguans had experienced seventeen wars in seventeen years, culminating in a bloody civil conflict. Ambitious warlords fought constant battles, obeying a traditional Nicaraguan proverb: "Power is like a woman who should never be shared." But in that year, the American Marines landed to impose order.

American Occupation of Nicaragua

For the next twenty-one years, American troops occupied Nicaragua. Nothing was done without consulting the American ambassador. In 1927 the American presidential emissary, Henry Stimson, told a Nicaraguan army officer, "General, the United States does not make mistakes."[5] "Praise be to God in heaven," went a satirical Nicaraguan saying, "and to the Yankee who represents Him on earth."[6]

The Nicaraguan relationship with the Yankees was complex. Nicaraguans were convinced that nothing could work in Nicaragua and that independence meant public depravity and anarchy. The Americans had provided peace. But they had also violated national pride and provoked resentment. Arturo Cruz, Jr., refers to the Nicaraguan's unique method of getting even: "At the end of the day, the Nicaraguans got their revenge in bed—by seducing an American's unfaithful wife. In the popular imagination, the first Somoza was the great avenger. They still talk about how this man, Anastasio Somoza, from the back country, found the keys to the heart and bedroom of Mrs. Hannah, the wife of the American minister. On the same chain glittered the key to power."[7]

Rise of the Sandinistas

After the Marines went home, the country yielded to the power of the Somoza family for forty-three years, supported by the National Guard, organized by the Americans to supervise elections. The Somozas were a corrupt lot, intimidating political opposition, encouraging corruption, and accumulating a vast fortune. His failure was evident in his handling of the Christmas earthquake of 1972, which killed 10,000 Nicaraguans, the aftermath of which I covered while working for NBC News. After the disaster, relief funds were shamelessly misused while downtown Managua lay in ruins. Blatant corruption alienated a majority of the population and sowed the seeds for revolution.

When the revolution finally came, America supported it. President Jimmy Carter cut off Somoza's supply of ammunition, arms, and gasoline. And the U.S. negotiated the resignation of the last Somoza leader. When the Sandinistas, in true Marxist-Leninist style, hijacked the legitimate uprising and revolution of the people, the President rushed a $75 million aid package through Congress to help the new government and gave active support to Nicaragua's credit applications in international lending institutions. During the next two years, America supplied an additional $120 million in aid and 100,000 tons of food—more help than any other country.

Yet Sandinista hostility to America was immediate. The new national anthem of Nicaragua included the line, "We shall fight against the Yankee, enemy of humanity." Within weeks of the fall of Somoza in 1979, the Sandinistas began sending arms to Marxist revolutionaries in neighboring El Salvador—a government the United States strongly supported. Salvadoran President Magana reported, "Armed subversion has but one launching pad: Nicaragua. While Nicaragua draws the attention of the world by saying they are on the verge of being invaded by the United States, they have not ceased for one instant to invade our country."[8]

It should have come as no surprise. The most important Sandinista leaders had all studied in Cuba or the Soviet Union. Interior Minister

Thomas Borges was trained to be a commander at a Cuban military school. Henry Ruiz studied for two years in Moscow and trained in the Middle East with the Palestine Liberation Organization. Humberto Ortega also received instruction in Cuba. This pattern continues. Nicaraguan security personnel are trained for two years in Cuba or three years in the USSR. Borges, in 1980, candidly stated, "I believe that it would be frivolous, and even dishonest, to say that no one here talks of Marxism-Leninism. I believe we are Marxists."[9]

As soon as the Sandinistas took power, they placed the state television system under Cuban managers. All Nicaraguan universities were "reformed" by a team of five Cuban specialists. Cuban military advisers arrived in Nicaragua on the day the Sandinistas seized power. Within a week there were one hundred Cuban advisors. Within three months there were several thousand. At the end of 1989, by some estimates, there were 3,000 Cuban military and security personnel in Nicaragua. The East Germans have provided trucks, police specialists, and communications technicians. The Bulgarians have helped with security. Czechoslovakia has provided weapons, explosives, and ammunition.

The Sandinistas have increased the size of their armed forces to nearly ten times the size of the Somoza National Guard. They have added thirty-six major military installations to the thirteen under Somoza. No wonder Ortega was so reluctant to relinquish this kind of power and control.

Political opposition to the Sandinistas was strictly controlled from the beginning. In 1981 the owner of the largest independent radio station in Nicaragua was beaten by government-organized mobs. The two radio stations were destroyed. The only independent opposition newspaper, *La Prensa,* was temporarily closed to protect its street vendors, mostly children. In the forty-three years of Somoza rule, *La Prensa* was shut down or censored nine times. The Sandinistas surpassed that figure before three years was up. But these actions were often excused by American supporters of the Sandinistas. One American religious leader commented, "People here are not so sophisticated, and no one minds if the government shuts down a newspaper occasionally."[10] The Sandinista secret police directed the so-called *turbas,* or divine mobs, which are used to suppress the political opposition, including efforts to embarrass and restrict the Pope on his visit to Managua, attacks on democratic electoral opponents, and attacks on independent labor leaders. Sandinista Defense Committees, based in neighborhoods, provided a network of informers and withheld passports, visas, and licenses from opponents of the Sandinistas. Robert Leiken reports, "One of the most common means of sustaining the myth of popular support is the Sandinistas' use of the rationing system as a lever. In numerous villages and cities, ration cards are confiscated for nonattendance at Sandinista meetings."[11]

In 1979 the Sandinistas promised free elections. But at one point in 1983, they had confined about 200 members of the largest non-Marxist political parties in jail for political activities. During sham elections in 1984, the government controlled the media, the balloting, and ballot-counting processes. Daniel Ortega won the election with 64 percent of the vote, almost the same margin as the Somozas used to get in rigged electoral contests. He earlier commented, "The elections that we are referring to are very different from the elections sought by the oligarchies and traitors. The elections imposed by the gringos will not be ours. Remember well that our elections shall be to strengthen revolutionary power, not raffle it off."[12] *The New York Times* reported that "only the naive believe that Sunday's election in Nicaragua was democratic or legitimizing proof of the Sandinistas' popularity."[13]

Economic mismanagement, bureaucratization, and a mounting defense budget have ruined the Nicaraguan economy. Gasoline, water, toilet paper, and a number of basic foodstuffs are now rationed.

While faltering on the economic front, the regime has been pushing ahead with "progressive" education — tailored to advance socialist transformation. In workshops for teachers, the education ministry uses material printed in Cuba and the USSR. Even publications aimed at very young children talk of the Sandinistas, the necessity of revolution, the armed forces, and hatred of the Yankees. For example, a mathematics primer teaches multiplication with illustrations of Soviet-made AK-47 rifles and hand grenades.

The Church and the Government

Perhaps most disturbing of all, the Sandinistas made a concerted attempt to divide and co-opt the church. In October 1979 the Sandinista party elite met behind closed doors to draft a post-victory strategy known as the Document of the Seventy-Two Hours. On the issue of the church, it reads:

> With the Catholic church, we should foster relations at the diplomatic level, observing a careful policy to neutralize the conservative stands and increase the links with priests open to the revolution, at the same time we promote the revolutionary sectors of the church. With the Protestant church we should implement a restrictive policy, developing intelligence surveillance on them, and, if they are caught off guard, expel them at once.[14]

A conscious attempt is made to reinterpret Christian symbols with revolutionary content. In its 1981 New Year's message, the Nicaraguan government stated: "The true Christians, the sincere Christians, embrace the option of the Sandinista revolution which today constitutes the option for the poor."[15] A Nicaraguan official was quoted as saying, "For me there is no Christian who is not a revolutionary. If somebody tells me that some priest is a good Christian and that he does not live the revolution, for me he is not a Christian; he is the opposite."[16] A policy statement by the "church of the poor"—or the government-allied church—argued in 1980: "The only way to love God, whom we do not see, is by contributing to the advancement of this revolutionary process in the most radical way possible. Only then shall we be loving our brothers, whom we do see. Therefore, we say that to be a Christian is to be a revolutionary."[17]

Margaret Randall, in her book on Christians in the revolution, provides a glimpse of what this means in practice. "Some days later I happened to witness a baptism celebrated by one of the four priests holding government office. 'Now we know,' he said, 'that original sin is the division of society into classes. . . . I command you, spirit of egoism, of capitalism, to come out of this child.' And while he poured the water on the forehead of the baby, he ended with, 'Now I give you your revolutionary membership.'"[18]

As early as the fall of 1979, the Sandinistas printed thousands of posters to commemorate Christmas as the advent of the "new man"—a Marxist term for the unselfish man born with socialism.

A May Day speech by commander Jaime Wheelock illustrates their approach. Referring to the Beatitudes, Wheelock asked,

Who is the one who said, "Blessed are the poor for they shall inherit the earth?" The crowd answered: "Jesus Christ." Wheelock then asked: "And who are the ones who fulfill these Christian principles in the most direct way?" And the people answered, "The Sandinistas." Wheelock concluded, "Therefore, there is no contradiction between Christianity and the revolution, and they could even say we are atheists. Well, let us admit it, that there are some inside the FSLN who, because of these ideas, their ideology, their study, have begun to think that God does not exist; let us admit it, but we shall not discuss this."[19]

The Future

The evidence is clear to everyone who has not deliberately closed his eyes so as not to see. From the beginning, the Sandinistas engaged in a pattern of political oppression of the unions, the political opposition, and the press. They attempted to subvert their neighbors and the church. By some estimates, over 10 percent of Nicaragua's population has left the country in their search for freedom.

But even with all of this evidence, and much more, many Christian leaders and lay people insisted on believing Sandinista promises, while ignoring Sandinista actions. A few years ago, two dozen bishops from major denominations formed a human chain across the steps of the United States Capitol, demanding an end to U.S. opposition to Nicaragua's Sandinista government. Episcopal Bishop Paul Moore said his own visits to the region had convinced him "that the Sandinistas were a duly elected, popularly supported, even Christian government."[20]

A group of professors from conservative Christian colleges, visiting Nicaragua, admitted seeing "some censorship and suppression of dissent." But they added, "such personal infringements are primarily the result of a state of defense against outside aggression in which the United States is playing a major role."

"We have confirmed," said the professors, "the essence of a government of the people, by the people, and for the people, including for the first time the very poor."[21]

Christians have rarely been known for their discernment in international politics. But this kind of blindness can cause great harm, particularly to those of like faith within Nicaragua. Almost fifty years ago,

Hewlett Johnson, a prominent Anglican clergyman and Dean of Canterbury, returned from a trip to the Soviet Union and described Joseph Stalin as "leading his people down new and unfamiliar avenues of democracy."[22] Another Christian leader reported of Stalin, "Never a man was more candid, fair, and honest — no one is afraid of him and everyone trusts him."[23] Still another was impressed by "his brown eyes, which are exceedingly wise and gentle."[24]

At the time, of course, Stalin was involved in a systematic campaign of mass murder. It is estimated that if all the victims of Stalin's terror were unearthed, twenty million skulls would bear witness to his firing squads and enforced famine. "The scandal," writes Robert Conquest, "is not that [Western opinion leaders] justified the Soviet actions, but that they refused to hear about them, that they were not prepared to face evidence."[25]

With momentous and still uncertain changes taking place in Eastern Europe, many religious leaders and groups took up the cause of peace and justice in Central America, particularly in Nicaragua. Having lost their influence by backing the wrong side, they are not expected to slow down, but to continue the pressure on the elected government in El Salvador to give in to the communist FMLN. But with Cuba announcing a cut off of military aid to the Sandinistas coupled with Soviet reluctance, at least for now, to bankroll surrogate revolutions, it is difficult to see how the FMLN will be able to continue its guerilla war at previous levels.

Still, the history of the political and religious left's involvement with Nicaragua needs to be remembered as another sad chapter in their and our history.

AT ISSUE

CENTRAL AMERICA

FORTY

THE PRESS' FATAL VISION

Hᴵɴᴅsɪɢʜᴛ, ᴡᴇ ᴀʀᴇ often reminded, is always 20–20, but foresight does not have to be blind. In the February 25 Nicaraguan election, there were far too many cases in which journalists were evidently blind or perhaps deliberately shut their eyes to evidence that produced a result they did not want.

Media Watch, a conservative media watchdog group that monitors the press and TV in its biweekly newsletters, compiled a list of some of the more laughable predictions about the election. While they are funny in retrospect, something like reading the predictions of astrologers and psychics that did not come true, they also display a clear bias.

On the February 21 "NBC Nightly News," for example, Ed Rabel said, "The election observers say the Bush Administration may have itself to blame for Daniel Ortega's rise in popularity among the voters. The reason, they say, is the U.S. military invasion of Panama. That was a move that was widely denounced here in Nicaragua. It was a close race until the U.S. invaded."

On election day, Rabel had a vision of the outcome: "Polls won't close here for another 30 minutes. But the widespread belief that the Sandinistas will prevail has shifted thinking far beyond the ballot box. The topic of the day is: How will a freely elected Sandinista government be treated by the United States?"

Even Ted Koppel, who normally is above such things, said on the February 23 "Nightline," "Almost certainly, the Sandinistas will win."

Peter Jennings said there was "not much to show" for the efforts of the Reagan and Bush administrations.

Other reporters canonized Daniel Ortega. Mark Uhlig of *The New York Times* wrote, "Perhaps the most striking aspect of the campaign has been Mr. Ortega's personal evolution from an unsmiling, often strident revolutionary leader to a polished, upbeat political performer who could as easily be a teen idol as a lifelong revolutionary."

CNN's Ronnie Lovler gushed, "One observer commented that Ortega will look back on this day as a turning point in his life, when he demonstrated to the world that the one-time guerrilla had truly become a statesman and a leader of his people."

She was half right. Ortega's defeat was certainly a turning point in his life.

This is shameful editorializing disguised as objective reporting and a disgrace to the profession. Who are these "observers" Rabel and Lovler refer to? They never say.

What is missing in journalism is more strident self-policing that could hold reporters accountable for gross negligence, crass editorializing, and blatant bias.

The Twentieth Century Fund, a private foundation, established the now-defunct National News Council in 1973 for just such a purpose. The council was comprised of private citizens and media people, but it went out of business in 1982 because the Twentieth Century Fund quit paying the bills after it saw that many in the press refused to participate. One of the built-in protections for the press was that complainants had to waive any claims to libel action for the council to listen to their beefs.

As one-time council member Ray Miller, former news director of KPRC-TV in Houston, recalls, "It investigated complaints against the press and filed a report which was usually published in *Columbia Journalism Review*. It had no real power, but it had the merit of giving people the perception they had some say."

The absence of that perception by the public has contributed to the growing arrogance and feeling of invincibility by the press. That arrogance and invincibility has led to a decline in press credibility.

It is in the interest of journalists—print and media—to resurrect the National News Council, or something like it, so that when the Ed Rabels, Ronnie Lovlers, and Mark Uhligs editorialize in the name of objective reporting, the complaints of the public will be heard.

AT ISSUE

CENTRAL AMERICA

FORTY-ONE

DOMINOES, ANYONE?

AFTER TEN YEARS of rancorous
debate over U.S. policy in Nicaragua, the celebration of last Sunday's
victory by Violeta Chamorro's UNO coalition party ought to continue
for at least a few more days. It's better than Mardi Gras, and this time
the Communists have the hangover.

If Academy Awards were to be handed out in the category of "best
policy designed to overthrow a Communist dictatorship and replace it
with a democratic system," the winners would have to be Ronald
Reagan, Oliver North, George Bush, Dan Quayle (who made four trips
to the region and delivered more speeches on the importance of the election than anyone else in the Administration), and a host of behind-scenes
activists on the National Security Council in the Reagan Administration,
including Jose Sorzano and Constantine Menges.

Each person kept the light of freedom burning while some congressional liberals attempted to snuff it out. For the likes of Sen. Chris Dodd
(D-Conn.) to claim that the election is a victory for their policies is a
greater rewrite of history than the textbooks used by the Sandinistas to
indoctrinate Nicaraguan children. The fact is that, without the continued
military pressure brought by the Contras with the support of the United
States, Daniel Ortega would never have agreed to free and fair elections.
To suggest otherwise is to believe that U.S. aid to the Afghanistan guerrillas had nothing to do with the Soviet decision to pull its troops out of
that country. But it's unsettling that President-for-less-than-two-more-

months Daniel Ortega is setting conditions for his relinquishing of power. He demands the immediate demobilization of the Contras before any "peaceful transition" to a new government. Any such decision should be the province of the Chamorro government. In a speech to his supporters, he said, "The day will come when we will return to governing the country. . . . In the meantime, we will continue governing from below."

Ortega also pledged to retain control over the 70,000-member army, the nation's security forces, and many government institutions. It sounds like a shadow government, something akin to a defeated American president living in the White House basement, plotting his return to power and secretly giving orders to the Joint Chiefs, while his successor occupies the Oval Office and family quarters.

It won't work and the Central American presidents, the Organization of American States, and the Bush Administration ought to make it clear that Ortega will not be allowed to drag his feet as he exits power. If Ortega had won, would there have been support for maintaining the Contras to make sure he did not further suppress the Nicaraguan people? Hardly. Editorial writers and the congressional liberals would have said, "The people have spoken, therefore, the opposition should cease."

Well, the people *have* spoken, and they spoke against Ortega and for Chamorro. If congressional liberals don't want to lift sanctions against South Africa until reforms to their liking are firmly in place, why should sanctions against Nicaragua be lifted until Chamorro's government has taken control?

The ideal situation, according to Constantine Menges, would be for the Contras to replace the Sandinista army. That would solve the security and stability problem immediately. But since that is not likely to happen, here is a more workable suggestion.

Let an international team of observers (Jimmy Carter, are you still available?) supervise a simultaneous demobilization of the Sandinista army and the Contras. Then, let a new army and police force be formed under the authority and direction of the elected civilian government.

As the leader of the opposition, Ortega will have many opportunities to make speeches and organize support for his policies and views in the national legislature. But he should do so based on the merit of those ideas, not on the strength of an army loyal only to him that could intimidate the freely elected leadership.

Having secured two major foreign policy victories—in Panama and Nicaragua—the Bush Administration is in a strong position to assist other nations in mopping up the hemisphere of dictatorial thugs and Communist guerrillas. With the arms pipeline to the FMLN Communist guerrillas in El Salvador severely damaged, now is the time to push for an immediate settlement between the Salvadoran government and the rebels. The Cristiani government should make it clear to the guerrillas that they will never be able to get a better deal than they can have right now if they will lay down their arms and negotiate for a peaceful transition back into civilian life.

When the history of this hemisphere is written, let it be noted that the Communist dominoes began falling when Ronald Reagan ordered the liberation of Grenada. That operation not only gave hope to other countries whose freedom was in jeopardy, it showed that American military power was still alive and in the right hands would be used to achieve legitimate objectives. The final domino is Cuba.

Gorbachev, man of the decade? Don't make me laugh. He is presiding over the ash heap of communism. They ought to be putting up statues of Ronald Reagan in Managua, Panama City, San Salvador, Grenada and, one day, Havana.

AT ISSUE

CENTRAL AMERICA

FORTY-TWO

PANAMA: BUSH'S FINEST HOUR – SO FAR

NEVER AGAIN WILL ANYONE be able to make the "wimp" label stick to President Bush, whose decisive action to restore freedom in Panama resembled nothing of the "tinny arf" of a lap dog that George Will once pinned on him, but instead resembled the deeper "woof" of a guard dog.

Cartoonist Garry Trudeau will have to let the President's "manhood" out of blind trust and begin drawing him as a person and not a disembodied spirit.

The real wimp turned out to be the braggart Manuel Noriega, who, after waving sabers and playing the macho role, ended his tyrannical career hiding behind the priestly skirts of the papal nuncio in Panama City, asking for sanctuary.

Whatever might be said about the Administration's unpreparedness, unprofessionalism, and uncertainty in dealing with Noriega in the past, Bush and his team proved that this time they were prepared, professional, and certain.

For the second time in this decade (in 1983, Grenada was the first), Daniel Ortega and Fidel Castro have to be wondering whether they might be next.

Let's hope so.

Noriega's surrender under the pressure of "Operation Just Cause" came at just the right time to silence liberals who have always been embarrassed by America's military and economic strength, and unwisely condemned the military incursion before seeing how successfully it would play out. Saul Landau of the leftist Institute for Policy Studies wrote in *The New York Times* that the Panama operation was about public relations, not the liberation of Panama from a crazed dictator and the installation of a duly elected government. The headline on the Landau column could have come from an old issue of *Pravda*: "Imperialism, Bush-Style," it said.

Washington Post columnist Colman McCarthy saw a greater evil in confronting evil than in its perpetuation: "The United States has been bullying and brutalizing Latin American nations at will," he wrote. This gross exaggeration ignored such brutalizations as the killing of civilians by the terrorist FMLN in El Salvador last month and the Sandinistas' systematic brutalization of the Miskito Indians over the last decade.

New York Times columnist Tom Wicker put on his blinders and wrote of "Those of us who fundamentally oppose U.S. intervention in other nations, particularly in this hemisphere." Notice the only country he mentioned whose intervention he opposes is the U.S. Nothing was said of the Soviet-Cuban-Nicaraguan intervention in this hemisphere.

As to the claim that the United States violated Panama's territorial sovereignty, that seems to carry little weight with the Panamanians, who are dancing in the streets, as their Grenadan neighbors did, thanking American troops for their national salvation.

The President, with the success of this operation, has greatly boosted his chances for re-election in 1992. Coupled with the credit he and the Reagan Administration can take for the incredible events in Eastern Europe, those '92 campaign commercials are going to bury anything a Democratic candidate can produce.

AT ISSUE

---

*ISRAEL
AND
THE MIDDLE EAST*

ISRAEL
AND THE MIDDLE EAST

M OST AMERICANS find the Middle East to be a mysterious tangle of unending feuds and unspeakable violence — a volatile mixture of ancient grudges and modern weapons. Periodically, when a new "peace plan" is floated, it is then sunk by stalemate. Often this is because at the heart of virtually every plan is a demand that Israel relinquish territory it occupied as a hedge against its very real enemies in the neighborhood, who have repeatedly pledged (and demonstrated) their willingness to obliterate Israel and the Jewish people from the region. These ideological descendants of Hitler would finish the job he began.

Occasionally an American hostage is taken or killed by terrorists who operate under obscure and ever changing names, and the region is front page news again. Eventually, though, attention wanes and the same confusion returns.

Any understanding of the Middle East must begin with the rejection of any concept of moral and political equivalency. All things and all people are not equal in the Middle East. (In the sight of God, they are equal. In the sight of each other and much of the world, they are not.) Israel exists because much of the world believed the Jewish people needed a homeland, their original homeland, as a hedge against another attempt to exterminate them as a people. Five wars have been fought with the express purpose of overwhelming Israel and pushing her people out to sea. Is it any wonder that Israel is reluctant to embrace socalled "peace plans" by other nations whose security, fate, and future are not at risk?

One cannot understand modern Israel or her justified paranoia apart from the Holocaust.

The Legacy of the Holocaust

In 1987, Chaim Herzog became the first Israeli head of state to visit Bergen-Belsen in West Germany, an infamous Nazi death camp. His speech was given on the site where over 50,000 Jews had been exterminated. West Germans, sensitive about their past, were hoping for words of reconciliation. But Herzog declared, "I do not bring forgiveness with me, nor forgetfulness. The only ones who can forgive are dead: The living have no right to forget."

Nazi hunter Gideon Hausner recalls, as though it were reported in yesterday's newspaper, "In Maidanek, Poland, there was only one place where the children were treated kindly: At the entrance to the gas chamber each was handed a sweet." At a museum in Jerusalem, there is a small glass case that contains only the soiled, crushed shoe of a child. It was found at the Treblinka death camp and preserved to ensure the survival of bitter memories. "In Israel," writes Aharon Appelfeld, "everyone carries a biography of the Holocaust deep inside him."

This harsh history has created a unique national character — vigorous and militant, but disfigured by suspicion and secrecy. Israel's attitude toward war and peace, diplomacy and negotiations, can be summarized simply: No horror is impossible. No one is to be trusted.

That distrust not only applies to enemies, but to allies as well. The United States supplies Israel with over three billion dollars in military and economic aid each year, more than it gives to any other nation. But the American government is seldom informed in advance of Israeli military raids, even when they concern American interests. No notice was given when Israel invaded Lebanon. No warning was given when Israel bombed an Iraqi nuclear plant. No notice was provided when commandos captured terrorist Sheik Abdul Obeid, even when the lives of American hostages were at risk.

Labor party leader and former Prime Minister Shimon Peres calls his own people, "divided, obstinate, and highly individualistic," a description that easily fits the Jews of Old Testament times ("stiff-necked people," God called them). They can seem bitter (one Israeli who survived the Holocaust is quoted as saying, "If you could lick my heart, it would poison you."[1]) They can be stubborn (during the six-day war, General Moshe Dyan asserted, "If we lose this war, I'll start another in my wife's name."[2]) They can be noble (Golda Meir said, "We do not rejoice in victories. We rejoice when a new kind of cotton is grown and when strawberries bloom in Israel."[3])

Israel's Neighbors

It is difficult to deal with an ally like Israel—a nation where wounds and suspicion run deep. But a few miles of desert across Israel's borders, an American observer moves from frustration to outraged incomprehension. The Arab world sometimes appears a very foreign place. The normal rules of morality do not seem to apply.

Syria's Minister of Defense, Mustafa Tlas, once honored a Syrian soldier for slaughtering "like sheep" twenty-eight "Jewish soldiers. . . . He killed three of them with an ax and decapitated them. . . . He fought with one of them face-to-face, laid down his ax, broke his neck, and devoured his flesh."[4]

In 1983, Syria sponsored ceremonies commemorating the tenth anniversary of the Yom Kippur War against Israel, heavily attended by civilian and military officials. Girls in uniform stood in a row holding live snakes. Suddenly, the girls started killing the snakes by biting through the snakes' heads. Next, young soldiers exited moving trucks and repeatedly stabbed a group of puppies. One soldier drank the puppies' blood, symbolizing the drinking of an enemy's blood.[5]

PLO gunman assassinated Jordan's prime minister in sin then drank his victim's blood.[6]

curial Moammar Khadafy once declared, "America's urned into lambs, and eating them is permitted."[7] Libyan radio, calling for attacks on United States targets, enjoined, "Oh, heroes of our Arab nation, let your missiles and suicide cells pursue American terrorist embassies and interests wherever they may be."[8]

In Iran the funeral of Ayatollah Khomeini was disrupted when mourners, in a religious frenzy, attempted to tear their dead leader's body apart. The corpse had to be evacuated by helicopter to keep it from being dismembered by Iranians intent on collecting relics.

When Americans pay attention to the Middle East at all, they see ancient, insoluble conflicts or images of irrational and gruesome violence. So, many simply refuse to notice, except in the most outrageous of circumstances. The United States sends about $5 billion annually in government aid just to Israel and Egypt and probably wishes the problem would go away. A majority of high school students cannot locate Israel on a map. Only half of college seniors know that the *Koran* is the sacred text of Islam. Nearly 15 percent actually identify it as the holy book of Jews!

The Root of Israeli Distrust

The history that produced these confusing Middle Eastern entities is a long one, going back to the earliest Biblical record, but one can understand nothing about the Middle East unless one knows at least some of that history.

In a 1985 address to the United Nations, Shimon Peres summarized it, "The sons of Abraham have become quarrelsome." But the present discontent is rooted in more recent events. It can be traced directly to World War II and the foundation of modern Israel in 1948.

Under the systematic genocide of the Nazis, one-third of the world Jewish population was exterminated. No other nation acted to save them. When Jews begged that Auschwitz be bombed by allied planes, they were told that bombs were needed for "essential" operations. Today, there are over twenty million more Japanese then before World War II. There are over fifteen million more Germans. But forty-five years after Hitler invaded Poland, there are still fewer Jews.

The war ended in 1945, but that did not end anti-Semitism and persecution. On July 5, 1946, in the Polish town of Kielce, a rumor th

Jews were engaged in the ritual sacrifices of Gentile children caused a riot, joined by the Communist police and army, which left forty Jews beaten to death. This, and other incidents, caused a stampede of illegal Jewish immigrants to Palestine, which was occupied by the British. Prime Minister David Ben Gurion commented on the influx, "Their faith is their passport."[9]

The Fight for a Homeland

In Palestine itself, radical Jewish groups began a terrorist campaign to drive out the British and form a Jewish state. On July 22, 1946, Jewish terrorists blew up Jerusalem's principal hotel, the King David, killing forty-one Arabs, twenty-eight British, seventeen Jews, and five others. On July 30 two British sergeants, captured by Jewish terrorists, were murdered in cold blood, and their bodies booby-trapped. Anti-Semitic riots erupted in London, Manchester, and Liverpool. From August 1945 to September 1947, 169 British were killed, along with 42 Arabs. Historian Paul Johnson comments, "This was a fateful development, because for the first time modern propaganda was combined with Leninist cell-structure and advanced technology to advance political aims through murder. During the next forty years, the example was to be followed all over the world. . . . The first to imitate the new techniques, naturally, were the Arabs."[10]

The British were forced to withdraw, but before they did, officers and soldiers conspired to give the Arabs supplies, posts, and weapons. Soon the Arab forces numbered nearly 30,000 Egyptians, Syrians, Jordanians, Iraqis, and Palestinians. The Haganah, the Jewish military organization, numbered about 21,000. And, at the beginning, they had virtually no guns, tanks, or aircraft.

In November of 1947 the American government pushed through the United Nations partition scheme that gave the Jewish people only 5,500 square miles in the Negev Desert. That amounted to one-sixth of one percent of lands inhabited by Arabs. But, confident of their military superiority, the Arab forces chose conflict. Ironically, the partition scheme would have given the Palestinians a good portion of the land they have tried but failed to obtain in five wars and which they now say they would accept (but Israel now refuses to give up absent iron-clad guarantees of peace).

Help for the Jews came from an unlikely source. The Soviet Union had been backing Israel to break up Britain's position in the Middle East. Now it ordered the Czechs to sell arms to the Jews. An entire military airfield was set aside to shuttle weapons to the Jewish forces in Tel Aviv. In April, David Ben Gurion was able to launch a pre-emptive strike, defeating the Arabs with Communist weapons. A month later, Israel was formally recognized by the United States. By December, it had a well-equipped army of 100,000.

Almost immediately an Arab refugee exodus from Palestine began. A primary reason was the massacre at the village of Deir Yassin, carried out by Jewish extremists. About 250 men, women, and children were murdered. Over the next few years, over half a million Arab refugees had left the new state of Israel. In addition, about the same number of Jews in ten Arab countries fled to Israel. By 1960 nearly all the Jewish refugees had been resettled. But the Arab states kept their refugees in camps, used, in Paul Johnson's words, as "human title-deeds to a Palestinian reconquest."[11]

At this point, all the elements of a continuing conflict were present. Israel was forced to defend a thin strip of resource-poor land against a coalition of hostile neighbors, championing the cause of Palestinian rights. (Golda Meir commented, "Let me tell you something that we have against Moses. He took us forty years through the desert in order to bring us to the one spot in the Middle East that has no oil."[12] And a large number of displaced Arabs remained in refugee camps — rich recruiting grounds for Palestinian terrorists, particularly the Palestine Liberation Organization. Referring to the militant PLO charter, Israeli Prime Minister Menachem Begin said, "Israel is the only country in the world against which there is a written document to the effect that it must disappear."[13]

In the four decades since its founding, Israel has been involved in five wars, none of her own choosing. Technically, Israel remains at war with each of her neighbors, except Egypt, with which she signed a peace treaty.

On May 19, 1967, Egyptian radio announced, "This is our chance, Arabs, to deal Israel a mortal blow of annihilation." On May 31, President Aref of Iraq declared, "Our goal is clear: to wipe Israel off the map." Despite protestations and promises to the contrary, despite public statements from various Arab and PLO leaders, this objective has never changed.

The chairman of the PLO, on June 1, 1967, emphasized, "The Jews of Palestine will have to leave." Arab forces, now heavily armed with Soviet weapons, outnumbered Israel's armies three-to-one. Israel's borders were nearly indefensible — at one point the entire country was ten miles across.

But on June 4 Israel launched another pre-emptive strike, routing Egyptian, Jordanian, and Syrian forces in a matter of six days. In Egypt's case, the loss was a humiliation. Israel occupied the Sinai, as well as the West Bank. And, most importantly, it gained control of Old Jerusalem, including the Wailing Wall and the Holy Places.

In October 1973 the process was repeated. On Yom Kippur, the Day of Atonement, Judaism's holiest day, Syrian and Egyptian forces attacked Israel. This time their initial success was considerable. A large portion of Israel's air force was destroyed. Important defensive lines were breached.

Prime Minister Golda Meir appealed to Washington for help. And soon $2.2 billion worth of America's latest weapons were on their way to Israel. Before the ceasefire was signed, Israel had recovered its lost territory and surrounded the Egyptian army. Israel had won. But the Arabs had recovered some prestige and remained defiant. Israeli Foreign Minister Abba Eban commented, "I think that this is the first war in history in which the victors sued for peace and the vanquished called for unconditional surrender."[14]

Prime Minister Golda Meir summarized the Israeli war experience, "We have always said that in our war with the Arabs, we had a secret weapon — no alternative. . . . The Egyptians could run to Egypt, the Syrians into Syria. The only place we could run was into the sea, and before we did that we might as well fight."[15]

Israel's Future

Modern Israel's future is uncertain. It is still a formidable military power, but the price paid for operating what much of the world views as a "garrison state" remains high. Israelis pay some of the world's highest taxes, which eat up about 70 percent of national income. Emigration and immigration rates are converging. One economist summarized Israel's economic policy as "being comes before well-being."[16] Over 30 percent of Israel's gross national product (GNP) goes for defense. The 1973 war consumed an entire year's GNP.

In addition, Israel for practical purposes remains an occupying power, though it is difficult to see how land on which their Biblical ancestors lived can be "occupied" by descendants of those first residents.

There are 700,000 Arabs on the West Bank whose average age is thirty and who are experiencing a high birth rate. On December 8, 1987, an Israeli truck hit two Arab vans at a Gaza Strip checkpoint, killing four Arabs. Rumors that the Israeli driver hit the Arabs intentionally set off demonstrations, which turned into rock-throwing riots all over the territories. Confrontation between young Palestinians, blocking streets, setting fires and throwing Molotov cocktails at Israeli border police and soldiers came to be known as the *intifada,* or uprising.

For Palestinians, *intifada* has become the expression of Palestinian nationalism. Israeli troops use tear gas, gunfire, curfews, and deportation to quell the demonstrations, but with little lasting success. The Israeli Defense Force reports a Palestinian casualty toll from December 1987 to May 1989 of 358 killed and 4,600 wounded, mostly as a result of Palestinian-initiated attacks on Israeli soldiers and Israeli civilians.

As a result, Israel is under increasing international pressure, especially from her "friend," the United States. The State Department, in its annual report on human rights, claimed that many of Israel's actions in the territories violate the Geneva Convention. Author Saul Bellow notes: "In this disorderly century refugees have fled from many countries. In India, in Africa, in Europe, millions of human beings have been put to flight, transported, enslaved, stampeded over borders, left to starve, but only the case of Palestinians is held to be permanently open. . . . What Switzerland is to winter holidays and the Dalmatian coast is to summer tourists, Israel and the Palestinians are to the West's need for justice — a sort of moral resort area."[17]

AT ISSUE

*ISRAEL
AND
THE MIDDLE EAST*

FORTY-THREE

DAVID AND GOLIATH
ROLES REVERSED

T HE LAST TIME I checked the Bib-
lical story of David and Goliath, David was the small Israeli shepherd
boy who faced seemingly impossible odds against the Philistines, led by
the overpowering giant, Goliath. With grit and ingenuity David won that
battle.

Critics of David's descendants have reversed the story and see tiny
Israel as the Goliath of the Middle East and the Palestinians in the role
of David.

If Israel is to be criticized for anything, it ought to be for its reluctance to clamp down more quickly on the disturbances that erupted in
the refugee camps and the Gaza Strip following rumors that a traffic
accident in which four Palestinians died was revenge for the stabbing of
an Israeli in Gaza.

That twenty-one died in the subsequent disturbances between Palestinians and Israeli troops is unfortunate, but the Molotov cocktails,
rocks, and bombs thrown by some of the demonstrators were not exactly
passive weapons. Nor does the death toll approach the more than 400
who died in the Iranian-inspired riots at Mecca. Arab criticism of the
Iranians was muted compared to the orchestrated outrage that always
seems to blare against Israel for attempting to walk the tightrope between individual liberties and very real security considerations.

An Israeli government spokesman told me that the demonstrations in Gaza were not as spontaneous as portrayed. Audio tapes made by Israeli security forces of conversations between PLO and other Arab factions outside of Israel and Arab activists in Gaza and West Bank reportedly document orders given by PLO operatives to stir up trouble. So again the Palestinian state issue catapulted back onto the front pages and television screens.

Bear in mind that Israel has had to manage the Palestinians because Egypt and Jordan have refused to do so. And the PLO apparently wants the Palestinians to remain in the camps, largely for political leverage. More than 100,000 Palestinians cross the Green Line between Israel and Gaza daily to work at jobs they never had before Israeli occupation of the region.

Without question the living conditions in Gaza and in the Palestinian refugee camps are poor. But much more has been accomplished since the 1967 war than during the years of Arab control in these areas and in the West Bank.

Institutions of higher learning have been established in Gaza and the West Bank where none existed prior to 1967. According to the United Nations, the quality of life in Gaza has improved considerably since 1967. Twenty years ago, few households in the region possessed such symbols of prosperity as refrigerators and television sets. Now, nearly three-quarters of the population own them. Fertility rates are up and mortality rates down, as is trade between the occupied territories and Jordan.

When Saudi Arabia's King Fahd called on Iran to join Arabs in trying to "liberate" Jerusalem, in spite of Tehran's oft repeated attacks on the Saudis' more moderate brand of Islam, it again revealed that underlying motive of most Arab states to push Israel into concessions that will ultimately undermine its security and threaten its existence.

As to the often heard criticism from liberal quarters that Israel uses excessive force to quell disturbances in areas it controls, one should reflect on a speech delivered by Associate Justice William Brennan at Hebrew University in Jerusalem during the recent disturbances.

Justice Brennan said it may well be Israel, not the United States, that provides the best hope for building a jurisprudence that can protect civil liberties against the demands of national security.

"For it is Israel," said Brennan, "that has been facing real and serious threats to its security for the last forty years and seems destined to continue facing such threats in the foreseeable future. The struggle to establish civil liberties against the backdrop of these security threats, while difficult, promises to build bulwarks of liberty that can endure the fears and frenzy of sudden danger—bulwarks to help guarantee that a nation fighting for its survival does not sacrifice those national values that make the fight worthwhile. . . . In this way, adversity may yet be the handmaiden of liberty."

In the Biblical account, David felled Goliath with a single stone from a slingshot. Israel's critics are trying to wear her down with an unrelenting fusillade of rancor. They will succeed only if Israel's friends, while not granting carte blanche to everything she does, fail to come to her defense.

AT ISSUE

ISRAEL
AND
THE MIDDLE EAST

FORTY - FOUR

THE PRESUMPTION OF ISRAEL'S GUILT

W E ARE IN THE MIDST of another of those frequent stormy cycles in which the presumption that it is only Israel's intransigence that prevents Jews and Arabs from making peace seems to be at the forefront of U.S. foreign policy statements. The latest storm began when Secretary of State James Baker delivered what many viewed as a harsh attack on Israel to the American Israeli Public Affairs Committee. And there were threats recently to send a U.S. emissary to Jerusalem to assess the status of promised elections in the West Bank and Gaza Strip in light of the decision by Prime Minister Yitzak Shamir's Likud bloc not to allow Palestinians from East Jerusalem to vote and to ban any creation of a Palestinian state, while continuing to build Jewish settlements in the territories.

The mistake some people make when viewing Israel and her Arab neighbors, the Palestine Liberation Organization, and the Palestinians is considering all these entities morally equivalent.

In fact, Israel is being pressured to negotiate with people who have signed the Covenant of the Islamic Resistance Movement, which is be-hind the *intifadeh,* or uprising, that began in the occupied territories in December 1987, and has been maintained with money and encourage-ment from the PLO and its friends ever since. No reasonable person who reads this covenant could expect Israel to negotiate with anyone who subscribes to it. "There is no solution for the Palestinian question except through Jihad (holy war)," says the covenant. "Initiatives, proposals, and international conferences are all a waste of time and vain endeavors."

While U.S. diplomats labor to pressure Israel into accepting a formula they think will bring peace to the region, the Islamic Resistance Covenant takes a cynical view of such efforts: ". . . the Islamic Resistance Movement does not consider these conferences capable of realising the demands, restoring the rights, or doing justice to the oppressed."

And what does the covenant define as justice for Palestinians?

"The Islamic Resistance Movement believes that the land of Palestine is an Islamic Waqf (holy site) consecrated for future Moslem generations until Judgment Day. It, *or any part of it,* should not be squandered; it, *or any part of it* (italics mine), should not be given up. Neither a single Arab country nor all Arab countries, neither any king nor president, nor all the kings and presidents, neither any organization nor all of them, be they Palestinian or Arab, possess the right to do that."

While Israel is required to deny intentions of a "greater Israel," no one demands that the PLO or any Arab nation renounce the "vision" of the Covenant of the Islamic Resistance Movement for a Palestine that requires a nonexistent Israel.

Adding to Israel's legitimate concerns is the growing arsenal of her Arab neighbors, all but one of which — Egypt — are still officially at war with Israel. While some Palestinian children throw rocks and other dangerous objects at Israeli soldiers, Syria, Saudi Arabia, Jordan, Libya, Iraq, and Kuwait silently, and without much publicity, build arsenals containing far more deadly weapons.

Between 1978 and 1988, Arab states exceeded Israel in military expenditures by more than $400 billion ($414 billion — $466 when Egypt is included — to $56 billion for Israel). The number of Arab forces now rivals that of the United States, with 3.6 million men, including reserves, under arms in Arab nations, compared to a paltry 645,000 in Israel.

In combat aircraft and tanks, Arab states outnumber Israel by a margin of four-to-one (Arab states have 2,804 combat planes and 16,685 tanks, to Israel's 592 planes and 3,790 tanks).

Israel's only advantage, its only hope of security, is the land that it holds. Have people forgotten why the land was taken in the first place?

It was because of five unprovoked attacks on Israel, aimed at fulfilling precisely those goals outlined in the Covenant of the Islamic Resistance Movement. Take part of the land without an ironclad commitment from all Arab states and the PLO to renounce their "holy" plans to eradicate the Jewish people and their state, and the groundwork for another Holocaust will have been prepared.

In view of the goals of the Covenant of the Islamic Resistance Movement, the pressure ought not to be on Israel, but on those who wrote and subscribe to the covenant to renounce it and replace it with a covenant of peaceful coexistence. Only then can meaningful negotiations toward a lasting peace begin.

EPILOGUE

In his classic book, *My Utmost for His Highest,* Oswald Chambers writes, "Life without war is impossible either in nature or in grace. The basis of physical, mental, moral, and spiritual life is antagonism. This is the open fact of life."

Here are some examples of the antagonistic mail I have received from total strangers. While some of it is incredibly personal, it serves as an affirmation to me that when one is on the right tract, he or she will be opposed. Rather than shrinking from criticism, one should welcome it as one of the signs that one is doing something of significance.

A Virginia woman writing the Washington television station where my commentaries are broadcast began her letter, "Gentlemen and other scum." She then proceeded to say that she would no longer watch the station because of my one commentary per week, which lasts about ninety seconds. This is what liberals mean when they use the word *tolerance.* For them it is a one-way street. Though their ideology is reflected universally, in news and entertainment, one ninety-second commentary is enough to send shivers down their intolerant spines.

Explaining why he would not take my column, the editorial page editor of a large newspaper in the Pacific Northwest responded to a reader: "A large portion of his columns in the past have been narrowly focused. We have interest in finding a columnist who can speak regularly on the impact of religious/philosophical values . . . on public policy . . . but Thomas strikes us as cemented into viewing such issues from a restricted part of the evangelical Protestant spectrum . . ."

That other journalists might be cemented in an agnostic foundation and express themselves from a restricted part of the liberal spectrum apparently does not concern this editor.

A board member of the Sioux Falls, South Dakota, chapter of the National Abortion Rights Action League said of me: "I think he's obnoxious. I think he's an ignoramus. Generally speaking, I don't think he's even a good writer."

Not all the mail is opposed to me or what I write. Occasionally there are letters like the one from a woman in suburban Detroit: "Yours is a reasoned and reasonable viewpoint of the issues which confront all of us, and I wanted to tell you that I appreciate your speaking out on these matters of concern to all Americans."

It is especially gratifying when someone of the stature of columnist George Will takes note of my work and understands what I am trying to do: "He is writing about the quality of life defined by things that are not material. He writes about the morals we breathe. He is a moral environmentalist."

The point in sharing some of my mail is to encourage you in your pursuit and defense of Truth. Opposition is as predictable as sunrise for those determined to take a stand against the prevailing spirit of the age. It is the lack of opposition that should concern us, not the level. In fact, the stronger the stand, the greater the level of opposition, and also the greater power one has for dealing with it.

Ted Koppel once observed that "Truth is not a polite tap on the shoulder. It is a howling reproach." People don't like being reproached, being told that what they believe in is based on a false worldview. Rather than consider the merit of an opposing opinion, they prefer the comfort of their own opinion and will attack the opposing opinion in hopes of silencing it.

Still, opposition should not concern us. Failure to present the Truth should. If this book, if these letters, have encouraged you to be bold in the presentation of Truth, then it will have fulfilled its purpose.

NOTES

Briefing: Abortion

1. 49 N.J. 22, 227A.2d 689 (1967).
2. "For the Record," *National Review,* September 1, 1989, 7.
3. George Will, *The Pursuit of Happiness and Other Sobering Thoughts* (New York: Harper Colophon, 1978) 61.
4. 410 U.S. 129 (1973).
5. R. Gardner, *Abortion: The Personal Dilemma* (Exeter: Paternoster, 1972) 62.
6. Philip Wylie, *The Magic Animal* (New York: Doubleday, 1968) 272.
7. Eugene Quay, "Abortion: Medical and Legal Foundations," *Georgetown Law Review* 1967, 395, 420.
8. J. Noonan, *The Morality of Abortion* (Cambridge: Harvard University Press, ed., 1970) 5.
9. Brown, "What the Supreme Court Didn't Know," *Human Life Review 2,* 1975, 12.
10. 410 U.S., 174–175.
11. Cited in Congressional Record, 94th Congress, March 3, 1976, 5108.
12. George Will, "The Case of the Unborn Patient," *The Pursuit of Virtue and Other Tory Notions* (New York: Touchstone, 1982) 110.
13. Ibid, 110.
14. Ibid, 109.
15. Don Colburn, *Washington Post Health,* October 18, 1988, 17.
16. Will, *The Pursuit of Virtue and Other Tory Notions,* 108.
17. George Will, *The Morning After* (New York: The Free Press, 1986) 167.
18. Charles Colson, "Abortion Clinic Obsolescence," *Christianity Today,* February 3, 1989, 72.
19. Ibid.
20. Ibid.
21. *U.S. News and World Report,* July 17, 1989, 18.
22. Will, *The Pursuit of Happiness and Other Sobering Thoughts,* 62–63.

Briefing: AIDS and Homosexuality

1. William Buckley, "AIDS: And Then What?," *National Review,* May 22, 1987, 56.
2. Charles Krauthammer, *Cutting Edges* (New York: Random House, 1985) 86.
3. Mike Sager, "The New Scarlet Letter: AIDS," *Washingtonian,* January 1986, 104.
4. Krauthammer, 86.
5. Pat Buchanan and J. Gordan Muir, "Gay Times and Diseases," *Orthodoxy* (New York: Harper and Row, 1987) 169.
6. Joseph Sobran, "The Politics of AIDS," *National Review,* 24.
7. Ibid, 24.
8. Michael Fumento, "Aids: Are Heterosexuals at Risk?", *Commentary,* November 1987, 26.
9. Ibid, 23.
10. Ibid, 23.
11. Sobran, 26.
12. Dave Walter, "Reagan's AIDS Commission," *Advocate,* September 1, 1987, 10.
13. Krauthammer, 83.
14. Fumento, 22.
15. Ibid, 23.
16. Ibid, 27.
17. Ibid, 26.
18. Ibid, 26.
19. Krauthammer, 84.
20. Buchanan, 170.
21. Ibid, 171.
22. Ibid, 171.
23. Ibid, 173.

Briefing: The Movies

1. Gerald Mast, *A Short History of the Movies,* (New York: Macmillian, 1986) 289.
2. Ibid, 430.
3. Richard Grenier, "The Hard Left and the Soft," *Commentary,* January 1984, 56.
4. David Brooks, "More Kafka than Capra," *National Review,* September 30, 1988, 29.
5. Grenier, 57.
6. Brooks, 29.
7. Ibid.
8. Ibid.
9. Ibid.
10. Grenier, 58.

11. James Wall, "Fighting the Media's Eroticizing of Violence," *The Christian Century,* October 3, 1984, 891.

12. Ibid.

13. Will, *The Morning After,* 100.

14. George Roche, *A World Without Heroes* (Hillsdale MI:Hillsdale College Press, 1987) 78.

15. Will, 101.

16. Ibid.

Briefing: The Making and Unmaking of Domestic Policy

1. Hedrick Smith, *The Power Game* (New York: Random House, 1988) xiv.

2. Robert Lichter, *The Media Elite* (Bethesda, MD: Adler and Adler, 1986) 17.

3. Lichter, 52.

4. Ibid, 17.

5. Ibid.

6. Robert Bork, *The Tempting of America* (New York: The Free Press, 1990) 340.

7. Bork, 341.

8. Ibid, 339.

9. Ibid.

10. Ibid.

11. Ibid, 342.

12. Ibid, 343.

13. Ibid, 283.

14. Ibid.

15. Ibid, 287.

16. Ibid, 342.

17. James B. Simpson, *Simpson's Contemporary Quotations* (Boston: Houghton Mifflin Company, 1988) 291.

Briefing: The Press

1. Lichter, *The Media Elite,* 1.

2. Ibid, 17.

3. Ibid, 27.

4. Ibid, 8.

5. Ibid, 23.

6. Ibid, 25.

7. Ibid, 294.

8. Ibid, 299.

9. Ibid, 14.

10. Ibid, 298.

11. Will, *The Pursuit of Happiness and Other Sobering Thoughts,* 81.

12. Roche, *A World Without Heroes,* 192.
13. Peter Berger, "Different Gospels," *This World,* Fall 1987, 9.
14. Lichter, 51.
15. Ibid.
16. Bill Kovach, "Too Much Opinion, at the Expense of Fact," *The New York Times,*September 13, 1989, Section A, page 31, column 1.
17. Ibid.

Briefing: The Supreme Court

1. *The Federalist,* No. 78.
2. "Essays of Brutus," *Antifederalist,* 2.9.189 in Storing ed.
3. Pat Buchanan, *Right From the Beginning* (Boston: Little, Brown, and Company, 1988) 344.
4. Bork, *The Tempting of America,* 54.
5. Bork, 41.
6. *New York Times,* August 10, 1964.
7. *New York Times,* June 16, 1964.
8. Bork, 178.
9. Joseph Sobran, "Pensees: Note for the Reactionary of Tomorrow," *National Review,* December 31, 1985, 55.
10. Bork, 69.
11. *The Court Years: 1939–1975* (New York: Random House, 1980) 127.
12. Sobran, 56.
13. Buchanan, 343.
14. George Will, *The New Season* (New York: Simon and Schuster, 1988) 157.
15. Will, *The Pursuit of Happiness and Other Sobering Thoughts,* 51.
16. Sobran, 57.
17. Bork, 114.
18. Ibid, 115.
19. Ibid, 115.
20. *Antifederalist,* 2.9.189 in Storing ed.
21. Bork, 190.
22. Ibid, 33.
23. Ibid.
24. Buchanan, 344.
25. Bork, 190.
26. George Will, *State Craft as Soul Craft* (New York: Simon and Schuster, 1983), 97.

Briefing: The Soviet Union

1. Paul Johnson, *Modern Times* (New York: Harper Colophon Books, 1983) 93.

2. Charles T. Baroch, "General Secretary Gorbachev's 'New Political Thinking,'" unpublished, 2.

3. George Will, "The Sickening Soviet Reality," *Newsweek*, January 19, 1987, 68.

4. Baroch, 16.

5. Jean-Francois Revel, *Commentary*, January 1989, 19.

6. Natan Sharansky, *Commentary*, March 1988, 29.

7. Baroch, 16.

Briefing: U.S. Foreign Policy

1. George Will, *The Pursuit of Virtue and Other Tory Notions* (NY: Simon and Schuster, 1982) 139.

2. George Will column on May 3, 1984.

3. Krauthammer, *Cutting Edges*, 158.

4. George Will column on May 3, 1984.

5. Ibid.

6. George Will column on November 20, 1983.

7. Krauthammer, 149.

8. Ibid.

9. George Will column on April 1, 1984.

10. Krauthammer, 150.

11. Ibid.

12. George Will column on November 20, 1983.

13. George Will column on September 18, 1983.

14. Krauthammer, 154.

15. Krauthammer, 159.

16. Ibid.

Briefing: Central America

1. Will, *The Morning After,* 300.

2. Ibid.

3. Ibid.

4. Humberto Belli, *Breaking Faith* (Westchester, IL: Crossway Books, 1985) xi.

5. Arturo J. Cruz, Jr., "Mr. Yankee Go Home," *Commentary*, August 1989, 48.

6. Cruz, 47.

7. Ibid, 48. 8.

8. John Norton Moore, *The Secret War in Central America* (Frederick, MD: University Publications of America, 1987) 29.

9. Jiri Valenta, "Sandinistas in Power," *Problems of Communism*, September-October, 1985, 8.

10. Belli, 91.

11. Robert S. Leiken, "Disillusion in Nicaragua," *Reader's Digest*, March 1985, 147.

12. Belli, 63.
13. Ibid, 69.
14. Ibid, 51.
15. Ibid, 140.
16. Ibid, 157.
17. Ibid, 156.
18. Ibid, 160.
19. Ibid, 143.
20. *The New York Times,* April 15, 1986.
21. "Declaration on United States/Nicaraguan Relations," August 5, 1983. Signed among others by Wayne Bragg of Wheaton College.
22. Johnson, *Modern Times,* 276.
23. Ibid.
24. Ibid.
25. Amos Perlmutter, "Misdeeds Rise from the Graves," *The New York Times,"* June 8, 1988.

Briefing: Israel and the Middle East

1. Will, *The Morning After,* 102.
2. *The New York Times,* April 12, 1987.
3. Simpson, *Simpson's Contemporary Quotations,* 9.
4. George Will's column of November 10, 1983.
5. Ibid.
6. Ibid.
7. *The New York Times,* June 15, 1986.
8. *Time,* April 17, 1986.
9. Johnson, *Modern Times,* 703.
10. Ibid, 482–483.
11. Ibid, 487.
12. *The New York Times,* June 10, 1973.
13. Statement to Press, March 22, 1978.
14. *The New York Times,* July 9, 1987.
15. *Life,* October 3, 1969.
16. Will, *The Pursuit of Happiness and Other Sobering Thoughts,* 274.
17. Ibid, 279.

INDEX

AUTHOR

CAL THOMAS WRITES a twice-weekly, nationally syndicated newspaper column distributed to more than 120 papers through the Los Angeles Times Syndicate. He is a veteran of twenty-nine years as a broadcast and print journalist and regularly contributes commentary to national radio and television news programs. He has worked for NBC News and Public Television and has won numerous reporting awards.

Thomas is the author of seven books, including, *The Death of Ethics in America* (Word), as well as *Occupied Territory* (Wolgemuth & Hyatt), *Liberals for Lunch* (Crossway Books), and the 1983 best seller, *Book Burning* (Crossway Books).

Mr. Thomas is a graduate of American University in Washington D.C. and has lectured or debated on more than seventy college campuses. He and his wife, Ray, who is a family therapist for the Minirth-Meirer-Byrd Clinic in Fairfax, Virginia, have four children and live just outside Washington D.C. in Manassas, Virginia.

The typeface for the text of this book is *Times Roman*. In 1930, typographer Stanley Morison joined the staff of *The Times* (London) to supervise design of a typeface for the reformatting of this renowned English daily. Morison had overseen type-library reforms at Cambridge University Press in 1925, but this new task would prove a formidable challenge despite a decade of experience in paleography, calligraphy, and typography. *Times New Roman* was credited as coming from Morison's original pencil renderings in the first years of the 1930s, but the typeface went through numerous changes under the scrutiny of a critical committee of dissatisfied *Times* staffers and editors. The resulting typeface, *Times Roman*, has been called the most used, most successful typeface of this century. The design is of enduring value to English and American printers and publishers, who choose the typeface for its readability and economy when run on today's high-speed presses.

Substantive Editing:
Michael S. Hyatt

Copy Editing:
Cindy Tripp

Cover Design:
Steve Diggs & Friends
Nashville, Tennessee

Page Composition:
Xerox Ventura Publisher
Printware 720 IQ Laser Printer

Printing and Binding:
Maple-Vail Book Manufacturing Group
York, Pennsylvania

Dust Jacket Printing:
Weber Graphics
Chicago, Illinois